NOW.

IS where DESTRUCTION
And CREATION
Come TOGETHER.
And FOREVER
REPEATS THE PROCESS.

NOWHERE EVERYWHERE © 2003 ISBN 0 9546361 0 4
Published by Yvonne Edwards, Axminster EX13 5AH
Printed by Creeds the Printers, Broadoak, Bridport DT6 5NL

UNIVERSE

UNI ---------- ONE
VERSE ------ CURVE

CREATION

A continuous movement
From SPIRIT -------- (outward breath)
To MATTER.

From MATTER
To SPIRIT
-------- (inward breath)

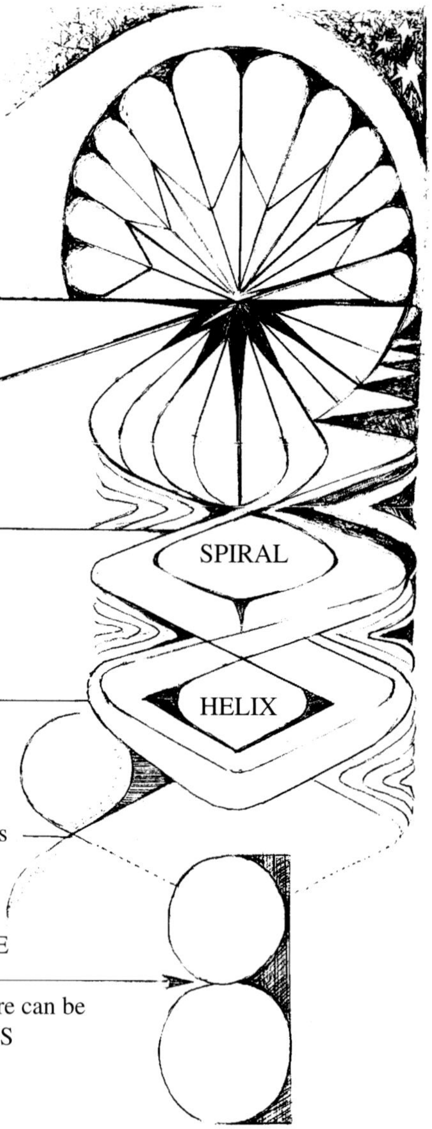

BEING

Is the ENERGY held together in
TRANSITION and in continual
TRANSFORMATION

COMMUNION

Is the essential sharing of BEING
It is the 2 spirals moving together
In the rhythm of TRANSFORMATION.
In its DUALITY the HELIX always faces
IN as it turns away.

LOVE

Is where it meets at a point of BALANCE
(UNITY)
Without that continuity of movement there can be
NO GROWTH …for we grow INWARDS
To a point of

INFINITY

Where ENERGY transcends to
ANOTHER DIMENSION . . .

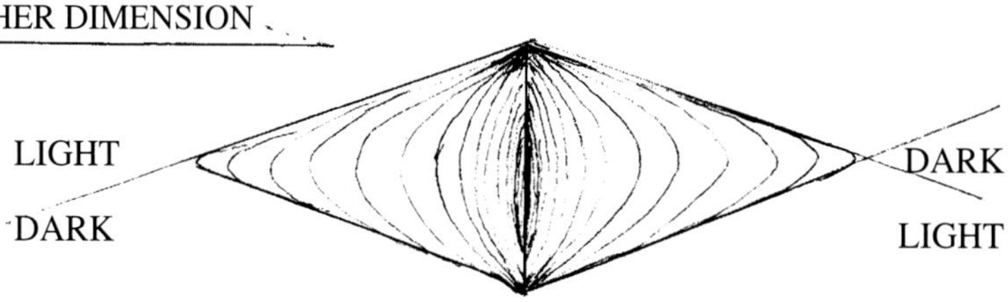

ZERO POINT

Where 2 spirals connect
(male / Female attributes are suspended)
MOTION CEASES so that new life can be CREATED.
Opposing / complimentary = CREATIVE SYMMETRY

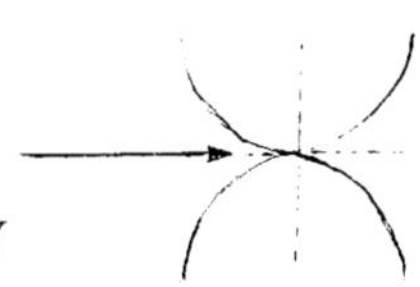

"BEING."

Is the Ever Repeating Design
That Stretches Beyond Time.
How Huge is the Thought
Wrapped in That One Word.

In
"BEING."

There is a need to Know Completeness.
That Great and the Small Are One,
For All that Exists
Is of the Same Substance.

In
"BEING."

There is a need to Know Consistency
In the Constancy of Change,
For Without Movement
There can be No Growth.

In
"BEING."

There is a need to Know Intensity
To Become as One Vibration
With the Immensity of Light,
That illuminates the Universe.

In
"BEING."

There is a need to Know Balance,
To Respond to the Rhythms
That Flow Forever Through us
In the Sameness of Breath.

"BEING"

Is the Elements in Harmony
Without and Within us
Giving In our Diversity,
A Unity of Purpose.

NOWHERE
THERE
EVERYWHERE.

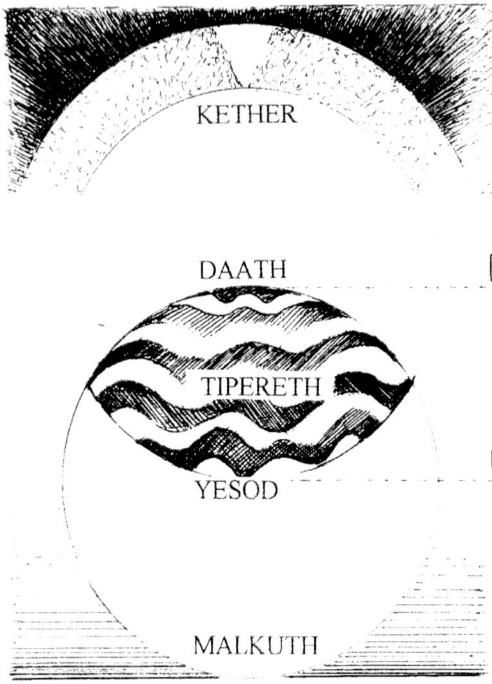

THE UNIVERSE.

INFINITE
UNITY
NOW!
LIGHTNESS.

SKYLINE

THE SEA

CONNECTING
UNCONSCIOUS
TO UNIVERSAL
CONSCIOUS.
TRANSITION.

SHORELINE

THE EARTH

DUALITY
DENSENESS.
HUMAN FORM.
DESIRES,DOUBTS.

THE UNIVERSE

INFINITY

SPIRIT

UNIVERSAL
CONSCIOUSNESS

UNITY-CERTAINTY

A Part Again of the
Universal Pattern

NOW

SUN

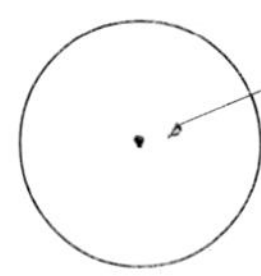

Point of Light,

The Aperture thro' which the Manifest (Man) is born out of the Unmanifest

THE SEA

FLUIDITY

THE UNCONSCIOUS

INTUITION

TRANSFORMATION

Movement between the Shore and Skyline

RECEPTIVE

MOON

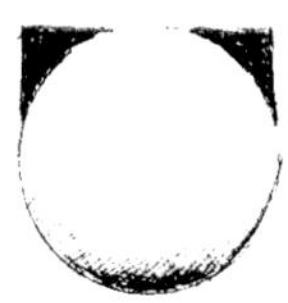

The Finite manifested Soul Link between Heaven & Earth. Absorbs Light/Heat From the Sun, giving Form to the Creative Force.

EARTH

SOLIDITY

EMOTIONS
SENSES

INSTINCT

DUALITY/DOUBT

Unity with the Universe Is divided between the Human Body/Mind (Senses/Emotions) And the Soul.

MATTER

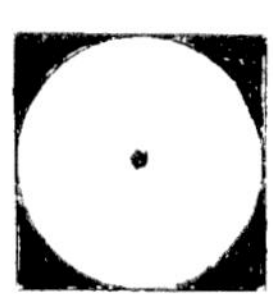

Encases Spirit, we have to free SELF from MATTER to liberate the Consciousness INTO Spirit.

This is a Place of Learning before we can Return to Unity. Lessons are given through going beyond the Limitations of The Senses and Emotions, and by "Tuning In" to the ELEMENTS, THE SEASONS, and THE UNIVERSE.

A THOUGHT FROM NOUGHT TO ONE!

In the liquid Language of Colours, Sounds and Symbols, this collection of Thoughts Mirrors the Voyage that we make through Life, for we are all unique Vessels, crafted to carry the Soul through the Wilderness that lies between Earth and Heaven.

As God Draws Breath to fill our Sails, we move into the Waters, and confident in our Infant Innocence, we confine our Soulmate that can navigate the starry Chart above, And Plough a straight Furrow to the Horizon, for It SEEMS so Near, but even as we Approach, It Withdraws, and Disappears into the Distance again.

So "The Game" goes on, a Conspiracy between Sea and Sky creating a perpetual Illusion, and in the confusion of these unknown Rules, we are laden down by doubts, The Sail shrinks to a hanging Shroud, and we sink in a trough of Despair.

In this Breath-Less Tomb of silent Walls, we hear our Soul calling us to descend in To the Hold and dispose of the Fear-Full Cargo that has stifled It for so long.

NOW, longing again for our Integrity we descend, scattering the Shadows to seek our Soul, and reunited in our Lightness the Sail unfurls to carry us on Waves of Peace Through the Final Horizon.

I GIVE THANKS FOR THOSE WHO HAVE JOURNEYED WITH ME, FOR IN THEIR EYES I SEE MY OWN REFLECTION, COMPANIONED BY ITS SHADOW.

So that your Intuition can guide you to the Image that you need, the pages have no Numbers.

THREADS OF THOUGHT.

From the frayed Fragments of the Garment
That masks Memory's true Meaning,
These Threads of Thought
Were Drawn Together
When a Friend asked,
"As You Stand on the Shore
Gazing Out to Sea,
What is Happening
Behind You
On the Land ?"
And through the haze
Of Salt-Glazed Eyes, I replied,
"I have been Here many Times Before,
Seeking to Reconcile Myself.
And though the Waves weave their Trappings
Around my Feet, to take them into the Web
That hides beneath the Tides of Time,
I stand unmoved by those circling Bands
That swell to surround Me ,and allow
The hard Shell that encases my Soul,
To dissolve through the surface of the Sand,
And come to rest on the Rocks Beneath.
And Anchored in that safe embrace,
I can look Beyond the Tapestry of Waves,
Whose dancing design blurs the Vision,
And in the Depths of that silent Space,
Listen only to the Inner Rhythm,
That Tunes the Truth of Earth and Heaven,
To One harmonious Whole!"

A GARMENT OF THOUGHT.

Thank You for Sharing with Me
A Fragment of Your Mystery.
For showing that Each Thread
Adds to the Fabric of My Being.
God give Me the Patience
To let You Weave This Garment
Into the Shape you want Me to be.

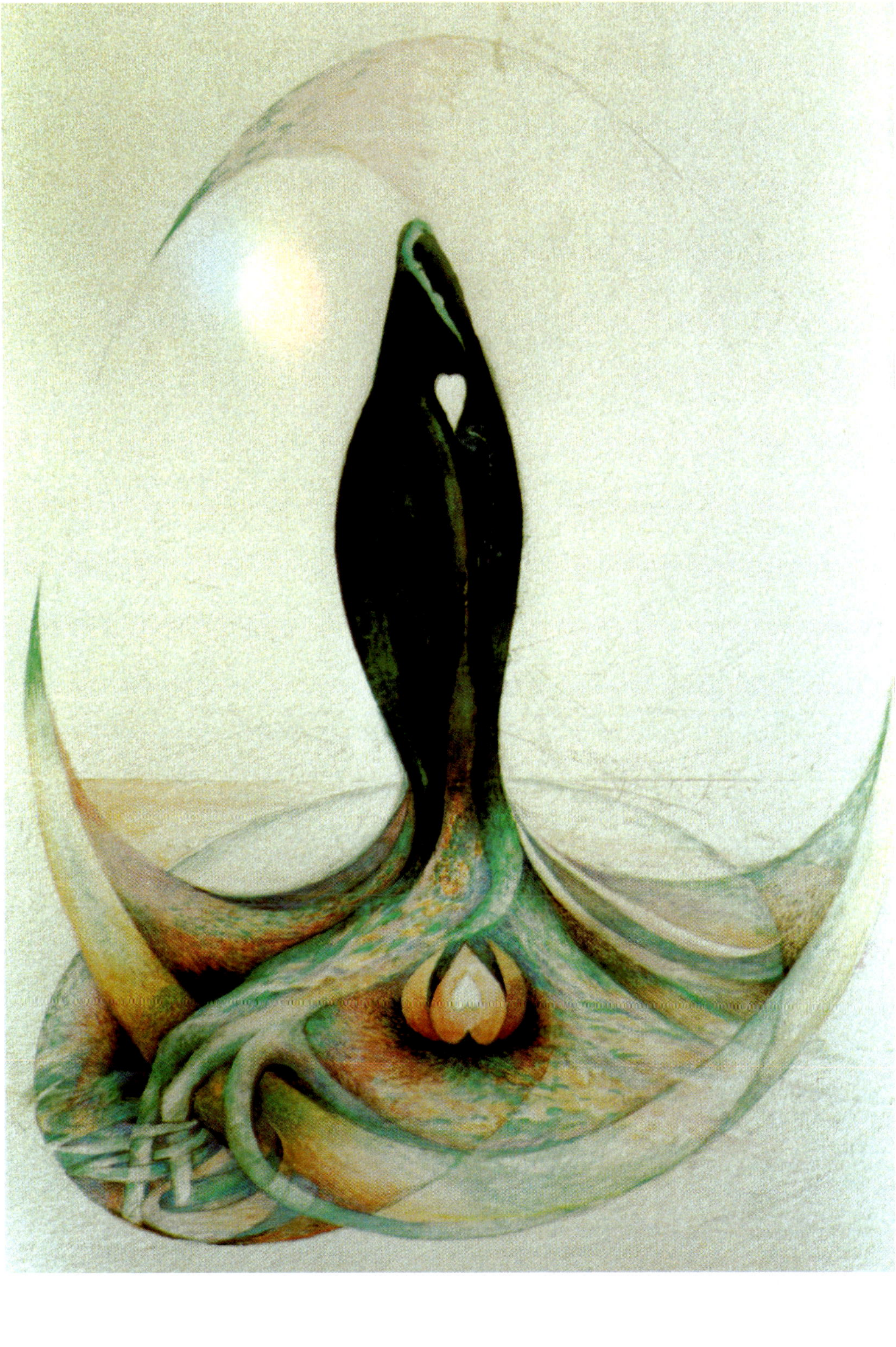

THE FIRST THOUGHT.

The Lord Created Me for the First of his Works
Long Ago, before all else that He Made.
I was formed in earliest Times,
At the Beginning before Earth itself.
I was Born when there were no Springs
Brimming with Water.
Before the Mountains were settled in their Place.
Before the Hills I was Born,
When as yet he had made neither Land or Streams
Nor the Mass of Earth's Soil.
When He set the Heavens in Place I was There,
When He girded the Ocean with the Horizon,
When He fixed the Canopy of Clouds overhead
And Confined the Springs of the Deep,
When He Prescribed Limits to the Sea
So that the Waters do not Transgress his Command,
When He made the Earth's Foundations firm.
Then I was at His side each day,
His darling and delight
Playing in His Presence continually,
Playing over His whole World,
While My delight was in Humanity.

(PROVERBS 8........22-31.)

A SHARED THOUGHT.

In Timeless Anticipation beyond Knowing,
I Sat in the Hollow Hand of Space, Gazing Out
To Gather In, and Return again In Darkness.

No One can show Me
The Nature of God.
I can See It in Others,
But don't Know It There.
To Know God,
I have to Look Within Myself,
By Myself, and For Myself,
By giving Truth the Freedom
To BE Everywhere
Within My Being.

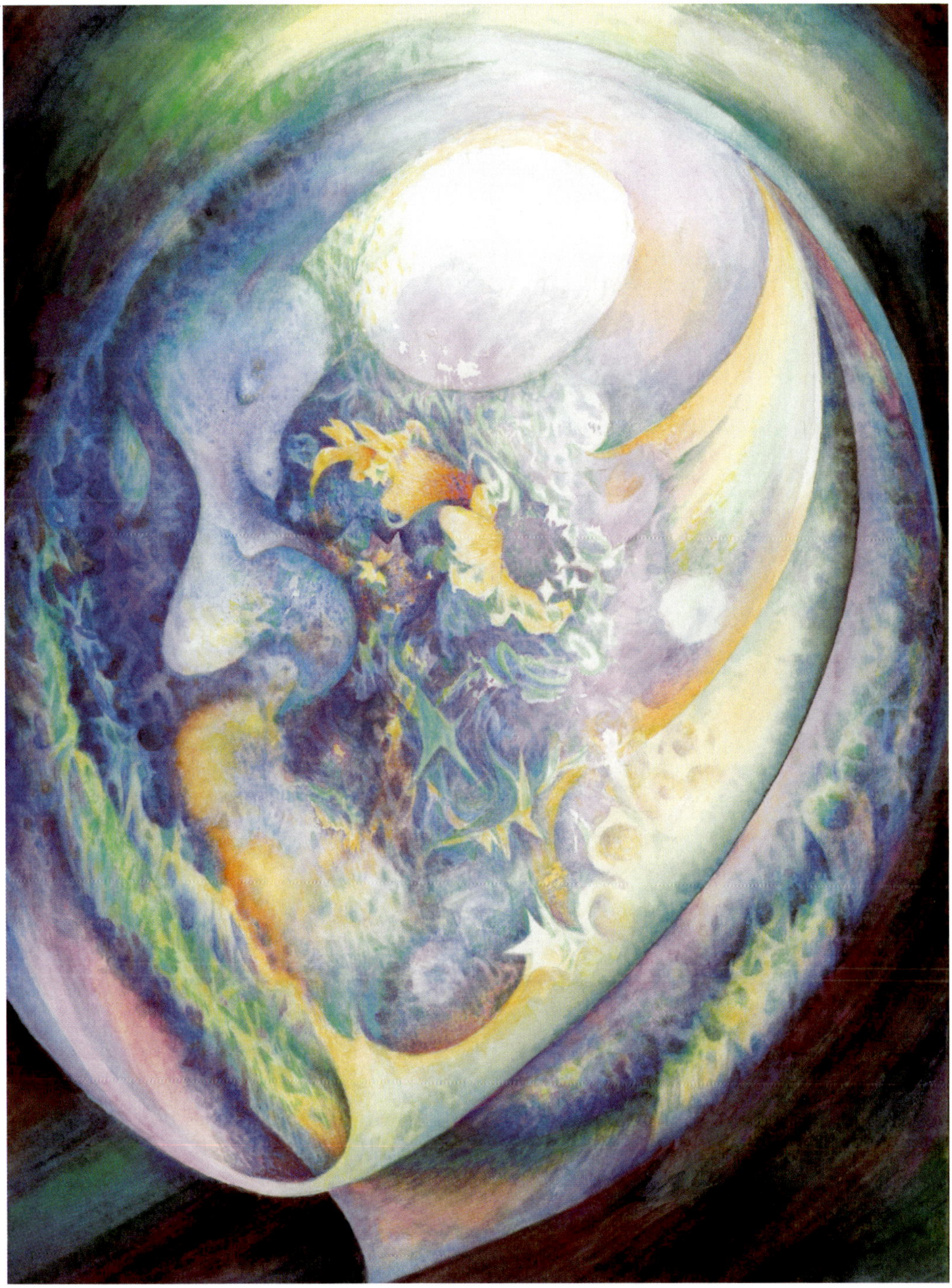

THE DAY OF JUDGEMENT.

I have carried the Weight of Accusing Words
Through the Narrow Passages of the Mind,
And as I passed through Its Turbulence
And Entered the Huge Halls of the Heart, I asked,
"Why am I Condemned for Being who I Be ?
I asked only to Be Accepted
In Darkness, as in Lightness
For that IS my Wholeness
That No Other has the Right to Take Apart."
And as I Knelt before the Altar
Within the Mighty Heart of Mystery,
An answer echoed down Its Aisles.
"Amidst the Darkness of your Humanity
You carry the Light of my Presence in You.
Know that the Sacred Seed of Life
Lies in the darkness of the Womb,
And though It grows in the Light,
Its Roots are forever Anchored in Darkness.
Know too, that Time and Space
Are but Barriers of the Mind
That Absolute Truth needs to Break Through
To continue on Its Journey.
Be not Dispirited, when Others
Clothed in the Dark Robes of Righteousness,
Pass Judgement upon You,
For their Intolerance is their Weakness Exposed.
You Know, that Wisdom and Compassion are Born in Suffering,
And Know too, that Inspiration, is the Child of Tribulation,
For Inspiration In Duality, is the Expiration of Divine Energy,
That is the key to My Paradox!
Listen only to My Echo
Calling you into the Depths of your Soul,
That you may be Refreshed in Its Cleansing Waters.
And as you Emerge from that Baptism,
You will Dance in Delight on the Shores of your Life,
Before Vesting again in your Mortal Clothes.
So Be Constant Always to the Integrity I Made You,
For that Is my Essence in your Being.
It is so Precious, so hold it Close in an Open Heart
That Others may Know Its Vitality.
But, allow No Other to Demand It from You,
For they will Burn in Its Intensity.
I Breathed into Your Nature My Generosity
That Others may Be Gracious in Its Sharing.
The Insight of my Vision I gave to You,
That You may Translate in Form and Light
That Longing to Belong, and give Illumination
On the Pathway Back to Me."

A FORGOTTEN THOUGHT.

As Always, lost
In the dreadful Darkness of the Night,
There Appear All Round tiny Pricks of Light,
Gleaning long lost Glimpses of Yesterday.
Where once, on the Fringes of Thought
Our spirits swept through the spreading Universe;
For There, God was Everywhere and Everything,
And we were constant Companions
In All that Existed!
But in Forever, Harmony could not hold Together,
And Dispersed as Threads of Light
To be swallowed into Darkness.
And from deep in its hollow Halls
God cried out in Sorrow,
"Even as I Love You, I have to Let You Go,
For My Creation needs to Grow Into Tomorrow.
And You can only Be There With Me
If I Sacrifice You In Today
By shaping You in Human Form.
But always Know in that seeming Exile,
I will Be There Beside You."

And in that cold Confinement, we Grew
And Knew the Corruption of Spirit Into SELF.
Where Controllers mouthed their falsehoods,
Saying that God created Man in His Image,
Even as we were told, to Create God in Our Image,
For how else could SELF esteem Its SELF?

And in this Time of Chaos
When the spirit sought its Freedom
From behind the frozen Mask of Self
God reached out, and held them both in his Love,
Saying "By Accepting the Certainty of your Divinity
Beyond the Fear of the Form I made You,
Only Then will you Comprehend
My Need Too, to Reveal Through You
My Creation, for you are but a Single Facet
Reflecting the Wonder of my Wholeness.
For the opening and the Folding
Of my infinite Facets
ARE the Rhythm of Creation,
How Else could It BE?"

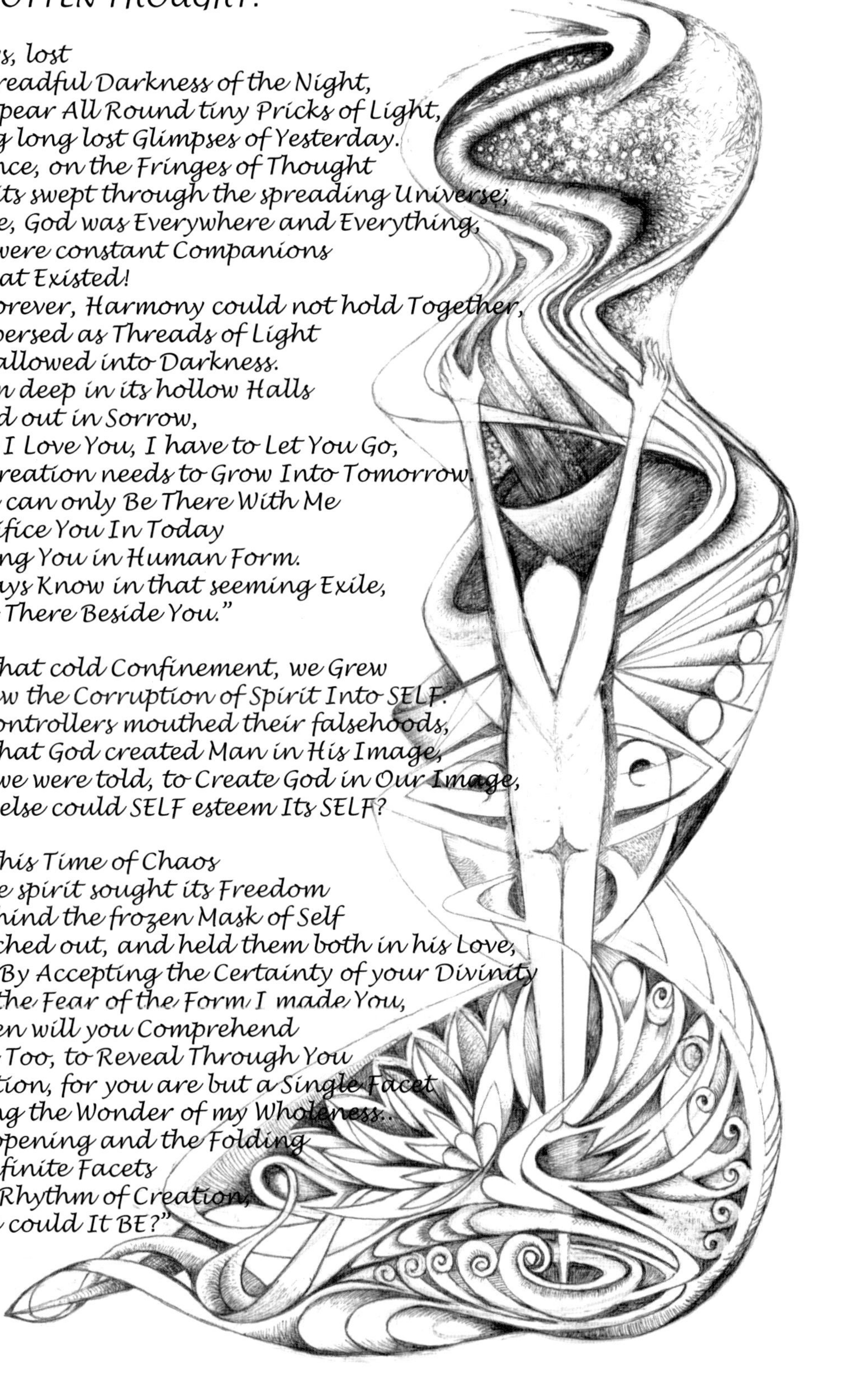

A GRAIN OF THOUGHT.

Now separated from their Source,
These shifting Sands of unformed Thoughts
Wander off, and are lost forever
In the Desert of the Drifting Mind.
But One Grain remains constant,
Contained within Its Self.
    And from Self came the Re- Cognition
    That I am Not the Whole Spirit,
    But only a Child of the Spirit,
    That has no direct Line of Return
    To My Moment of Conception.
And defined inside that awesome Thought
Was the need to find a passage back.
How hard it was to make the right Decision
When tempted by the offer of the upright Ladder,
Yet knowing in the deception of a straight Ascent
I had not the strength to climb
But in Vertigo would Fall Forever
And sever Connection to My Source.
    And hidden in that dreadful thought
    I Knew My Self, and choose instead
    To step into the slow progression of the Spiral
And carried on Its generous Back
I'm taken into the Darkness of Its Eclipse
Knowing that as I slow around Its Curve
I will Flow again into the Light beyond.
    And so in Its ever tightening Lips
    I'm Drawn into Its next Breath,
    And in this Pause the Spiral Smiles
    And Opens, before Descending on Itself
    And Leave me back at my Source.

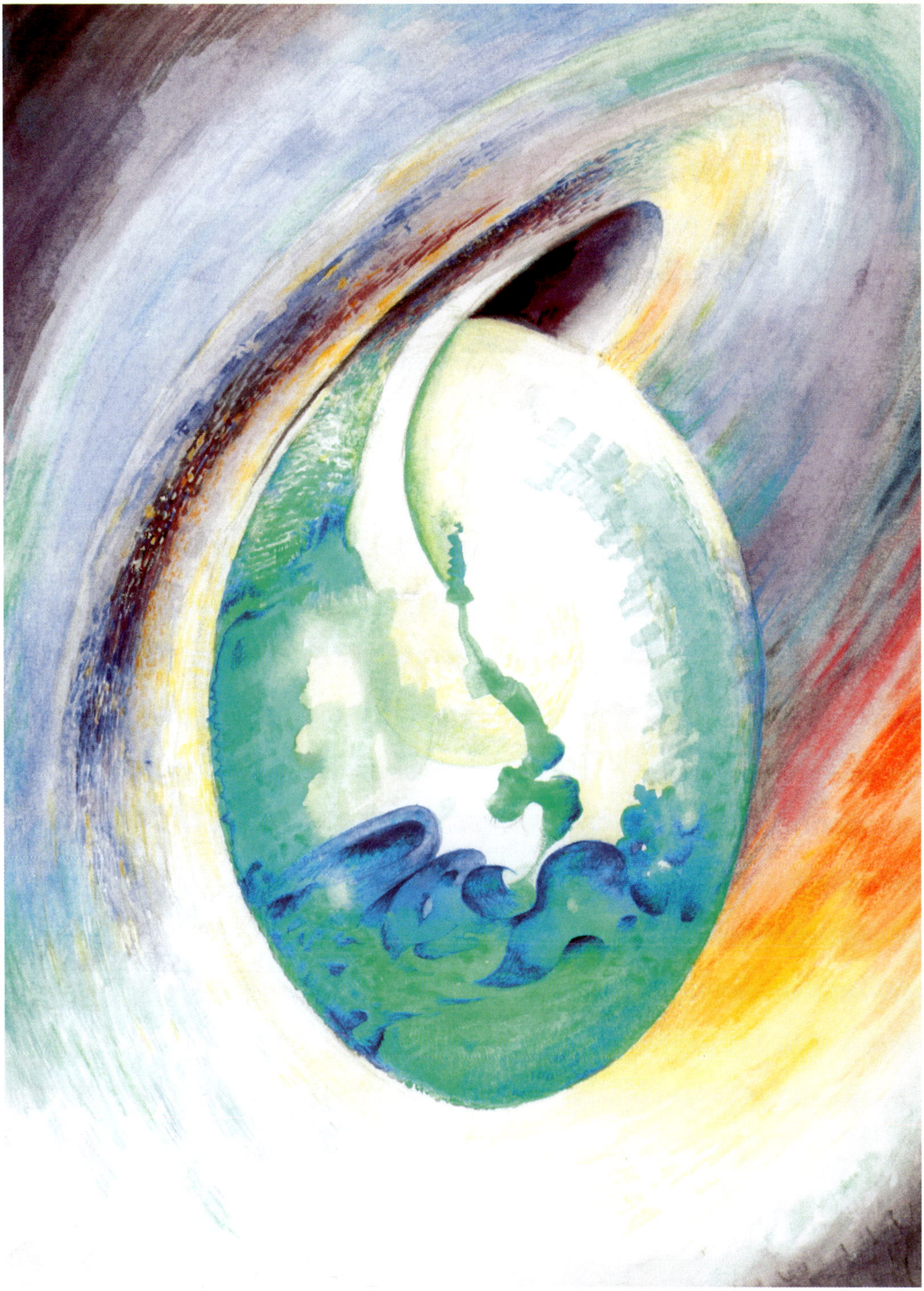

A SACK OF THOUGHTS.

As a Trysting Place God Gave us Dreams,
Where Today's Fears Can be Reshaped
From their Leaden Weight
To transmute to the Truth of Golden Ideas.
As we Descend Again
Into the Darkness of "Being"
We carry with us a Sack of Time,
To fill Its Emptiness with our Dreams.
Some choose to make It a rucksack,
As a Holder for their Hoarding,
And corded tightly to their Back
They stuff their Sack with This and That,
Like mesmerised Magpies picking Tit-Bits,
That flit without Dreams from Here to There,
Unaware, that their Gleaning
Of those seemingly gleaming Gems
Has hemmed their flow of Flight to Light
Into the Night-Tight Shrouds within their Sack.
And trapped in those Layers of Self Deception,
They Scratch through the Scraps of their thieved Collection
Seeking for Any Thing worth retrieving, and finding No Thing,
Shrink resigned, to be Buried Unmourned in their Sack of Time.
Some choose their Sack Be an Open Net,
Cast out from the Confines of the Mind
To Unwind as a web of infinite Threads
And Catch the Illusion of Time; whose constant Transition
Is the subtle division between Recall and Renewal.
And Trawling through Shoals of drifting Dreams,
They sift the Harvest through their mesh,
To Thresh the Essence of Thought and Feeling,
And give Meaning to "Things" yet Unseen.
From submerged Shapes strong strands are drawn,
Currents converge, and Visions Form, Gestating Ideas
That wait, impatient to be Born, and give Expression
To the Lesson that they Bring
For they had Known the razoring of Refinement
In the tight Confinement of their Sack, and uncomplaining,
Suffered the hurt of their Growing Pains.
But as they moved within Its Darkness, they had Known too,
The Love that had conceived them,
And in the flow of Breaking Waters
They perceived themselves as "Beings Divine"
Breed beyond the Reach of Time.

WHAT A THOUGHT!

Crucifixion and Resurrection
Are but symbols that Give Perception
To the Paradox of Who we Are.
For Entombed in the Womb,
The Spirit is a Chrysalis
Waiting Release from Its Confinement
To Fly free on Its Preordained Course.
And Within the Tomb
The Spirit is a Chrysalis
Waiting to Return from whence It came,
Carrying with it the Experience
Of that Painful Journey.

Held within the Container of the Spirit
Is the Allness of the Elements.
It is of Water, that always holds Level
Whatever Shape Confines It's movement.
It is of Fire, that gives Vitality
To Keep it's Entity Alight.
It is of Air, that Floats in Thoughts
Even as they Dispute amongst Themselves.
It is of the Earth, that holds us steady
Until we are ready to take our journey to its End.
For the Beginning Is the End
That Transcends Again!

In the Foliating of the Earth,
I Am in Every Space between
The shaping of the Leaves.
In the eternal flowing of the Water,
I Am the Pause
Before the random Patterns Re Form.
In the Transparency of the Air,
I Am the silent Space
That Holds its breath
Before departing Into Itself.
In the Fullness of the Fire,
I Am the hidden Spark
That Fires the Movement of the Universe.
In My Creativity, I AM!

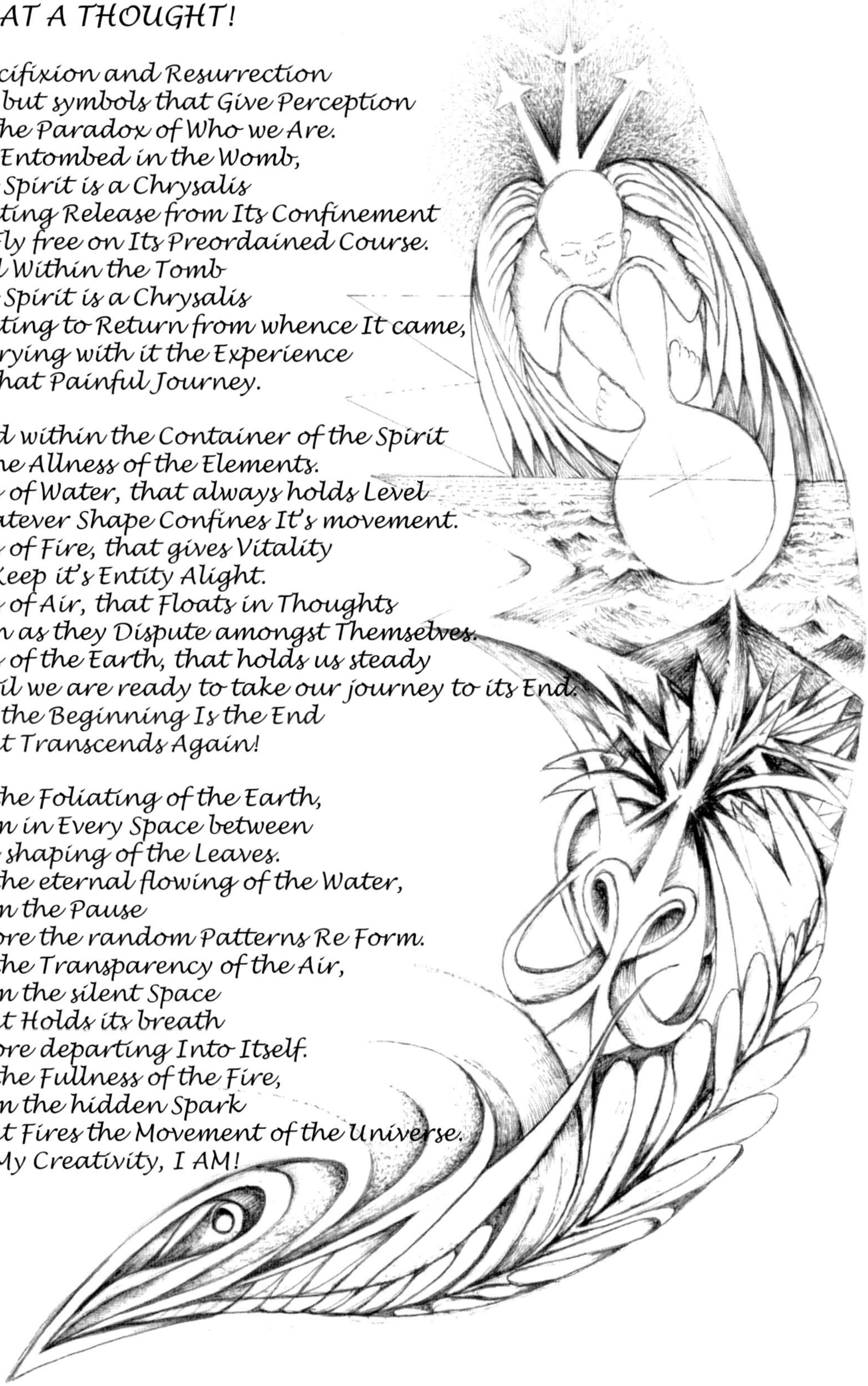

"A BREATH OF AIR."

GENESIS 1, 1-2.

In the Beginning God Created the Heaven and the Earth
And the Earth was without Form, and Void;
And Darkness was upon the Face of the Deep.
And the Spirit of God Moved upon the Face of the Waters.

God's Breath is given as Our Inspiration
Bringing Life to our Being in its Transformation.
As the Wind winds Waves of Exultation
From unbounded Sound to Pure Vibration,
That return to God in their Expiration.

From within his Perfection, God cried,
"In my need to Know My Self
I have to share my Inner Light,
For my manifestation can only BE
In the Seeing of My Reflection."
And God drew the Elements into Harmony,
And Shed his Light on the Ceaseless Sea,
Creasing his Breath as pulsating Waves
That swept the Shores of Eternity.
And as the Waters formed,
They swelled, and fell to cleanse
The Darkness of their Depths.
And in their next upsurge of breath,
They rose as transparent Wings of Light
Circling through the Music of the Spheres,
That in the rainbow of their falling Tears
Carried the ringing Trumpet's call
To awaken the radiant Spark of Fire,
Whose Zest gave warmth and Light,
And brought Life to the waiting Earth.
And in the softness of her Green Fingers,
She suckered and shaped
That which she had Conceived,
And from the fruit of her Labour grew
A glimmering Image of Its Creator,
A Being of triumphant Truth.

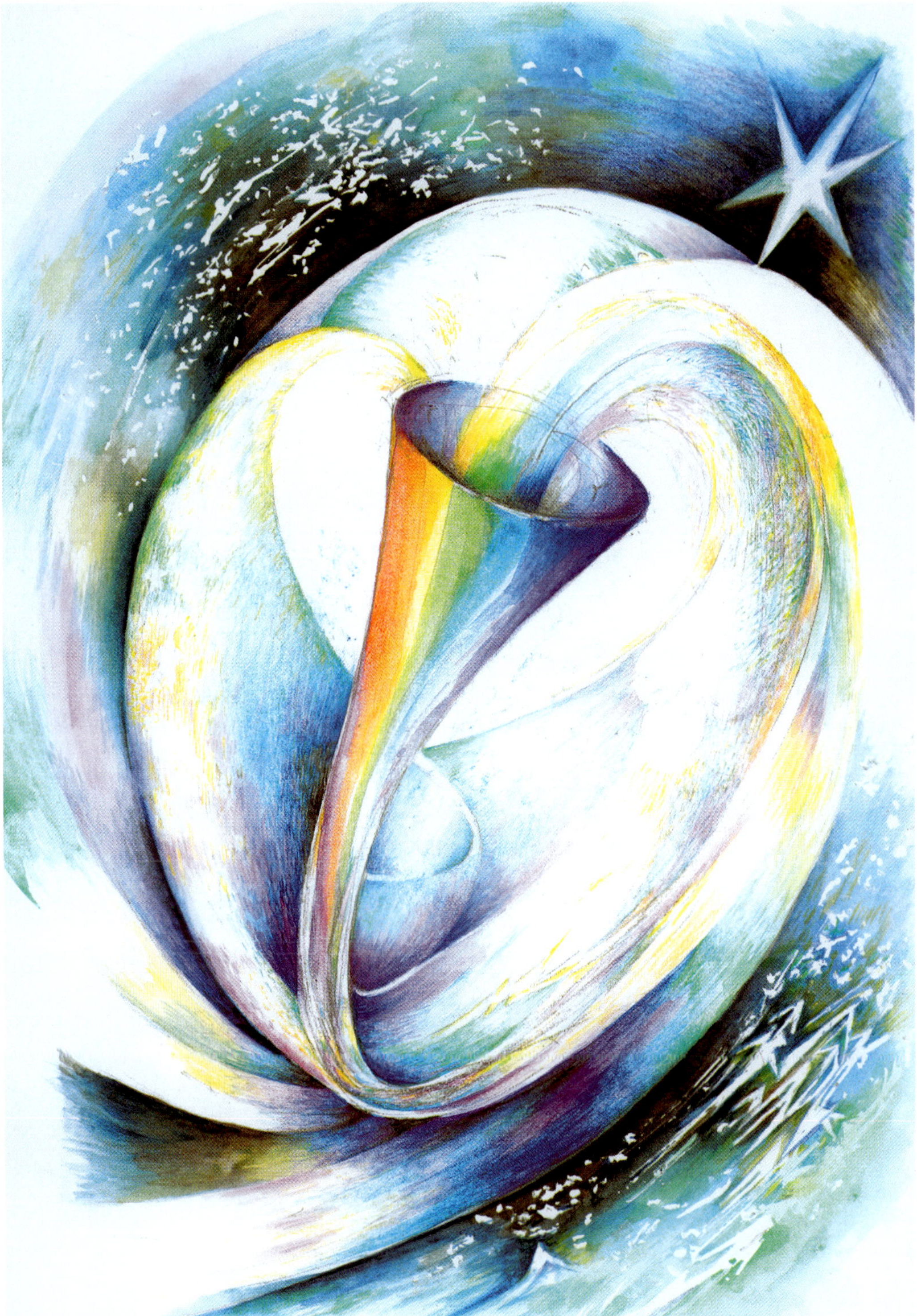

A TOWER OF SAND.

*And they said, Go to, let us build us a City and a Tower, whose Top
May reach unto Heaven; and let us make us a Name, lest we be
Scattered abroad upon the Face of the Whole Earth.
And the Lord came down to see the City and the Tower,
Which the Children of Men had builded, and the Lord said,
Behold, the people is One, and they all have one Language;
And this they begin to do; and now Nothing will be restrained
From them, which they have Imagined to Do.
Go to, let us go down, and there confound their Language,
That they may not understand one another's Speech.*
(GENESIS 11. 4-7)

Formed in the Fire of the Universe,
I thought Myself Invincible,
And Stood Aloof
In the Certainty of my Permanence.
I too, was a great Tower of Rock
That Intruded Its proud Spire
To pierce the Fabric of the Heavens.
And the Creator cried in his Hurt,
"The Cloak that You try to Tear
Is There to Conceal My Mystery.
You Forget, that in your Formation
You were but a Speck of Dust
In the Depths of My Manifestation."
And in the Severity of his Love for Me,
He Threw my Substance to the Elements
Saying, "I Loosen My Hold on Their Might,
That they may Re-Grind You
To the Shape I had in Mind for You.
To wear away that Pinnacle of Pride,
And take You into the Desert
As a Humble Grain of Sand.
And There without Identity
You will Know In Your Smallness
The Greatness that You Hold.
For only Then, can I Lift You to Me,
And Re-Shape You again In My Love."

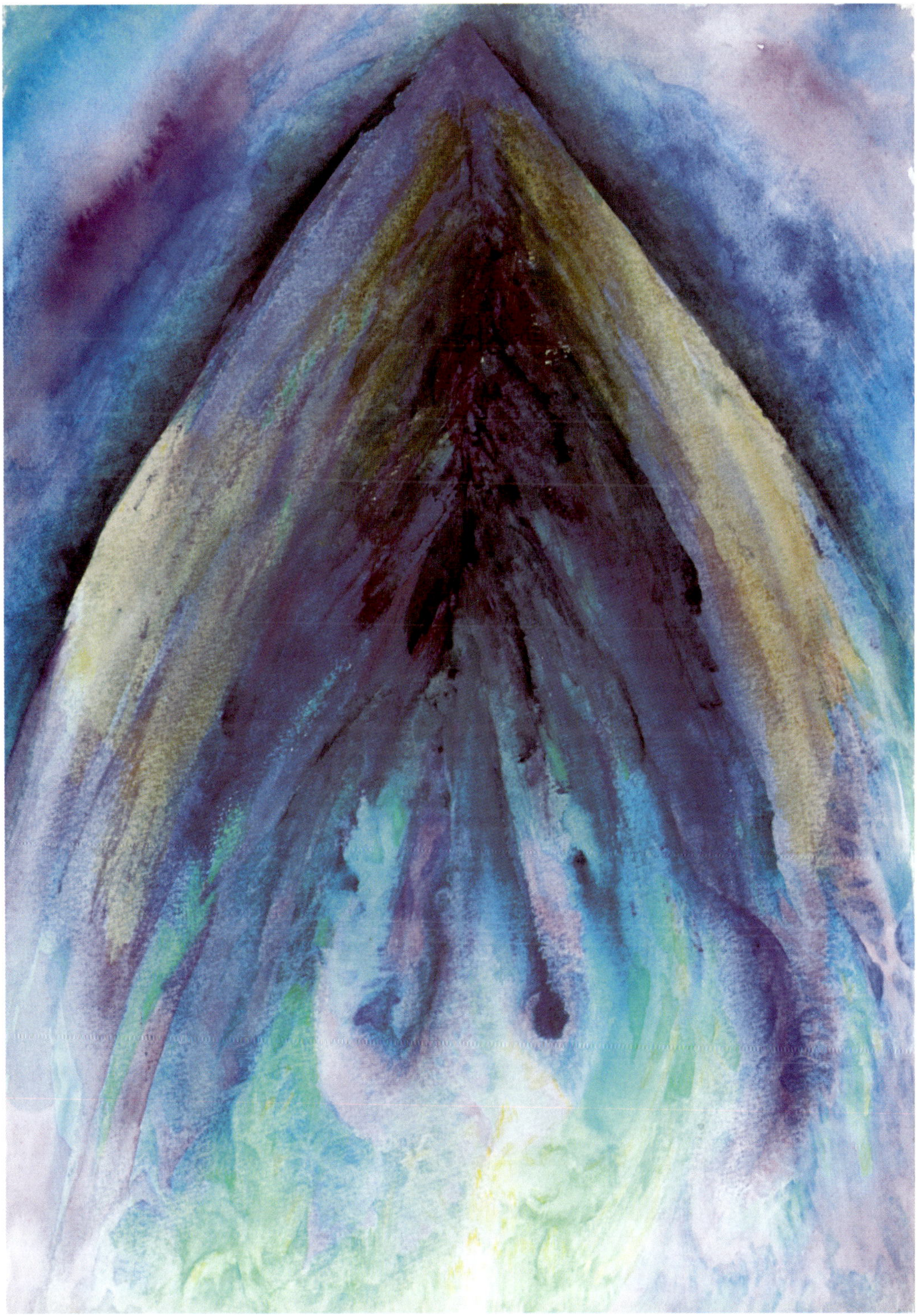

THE SPARK OF FIRE.

"AND GOD CREATED MAN IN HIS OWN IMAGE".

From the blackened Core of the Endless Void,
God cast a Shadow of Himself.
And from Its Greyness drew All Colours,
As a Blade of pure White Light
To pierce the Womb of the Earth.

And there he Stirred them to Procreation,
Blending the diversity of their Vibrations,
To Become A Spark of Life.

And the infant Spark, uncertain of Its Power,
Played with the colours stored within
To learn of the hidden strength they hold.
And being as yet a Child,
It chose rowdy Red and Glowing Gold,
And on their Rays raced through the Air
To Become A Flame,
That Roared in Delight
At Its Own Being!
But in the Intensity of Its Being,
It Lost Control,
Burning as a Pyre of Yellowing Fears,
And at Its Centre, the Heart Quickened,
And shed Tears of Light
To guide the Soul through Its Dark Night
Into the Peace of a Field of Green.
Here the spent Colours were laid to Rest,
As the Spark took Breath from the Blue above
That talked in Tones of Truth and Love,
Distilling again as the Violet Flame,
At One with Its Creator.

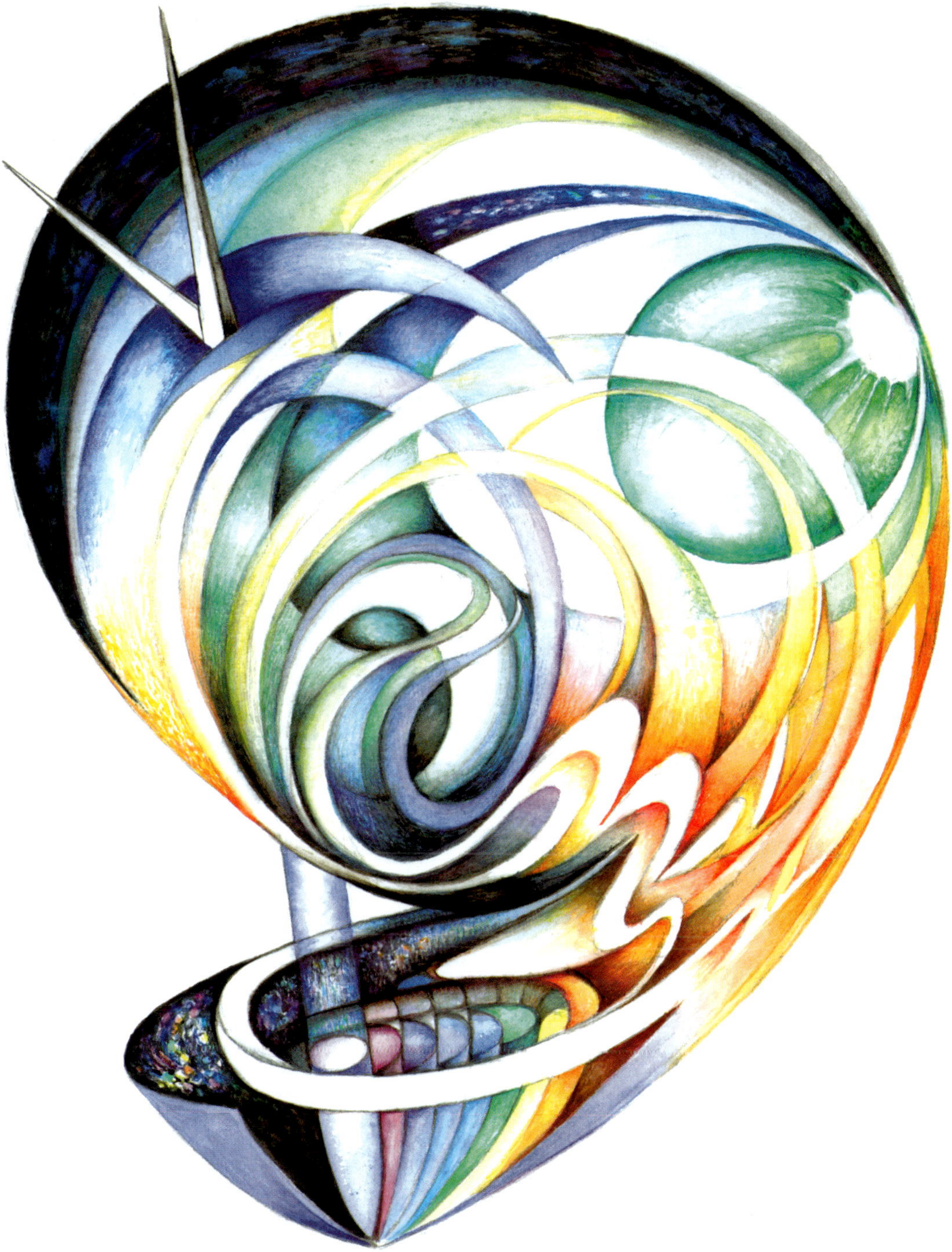

THE SPEAKING WATERS.

"The Voice of the Lord
is Upon the Face of the Waters.
(PSALM 29....1-3.)

And God said,
"I Will Speak With You
Through the Heart of the Hanging Clouds
That in the Fullness of their falling Tears,
Weep their Essence to Refresh the Earth.
So Stay Awhile,
And Hear what I have to Say."

And God said,
"I Will Speak With You
Through the Eye of the Clinging Raindrop
That gives a Glimpse of my Immensity
In the Transitory Hold of Its Tiny Hand.
So Stay Awhile,
And Hear what I have to Say."

And God said,
" I Will Speak With You
Through the writhing Limbs of the Livening Stream
That are Torn Apart in their sparkling Intimacy,
Even as they Fold to Hold each Other.
So Stay Awhile,
And Hear what I have to Say."

And God Said,
" I Will Speak With You
In the Reflections of the Shrinking Puddle,
That Dragged Down into the Sodden Earth,
Sags in the Uncertainty of Its Shape.
So Stay Awhile,
And Hear what I have to Say."

And God Said,
" I Will Speak With You
Across the Rough Canvas of the Silent Sea,
Even as the Moon Beckons to turn Its Tides
And Loosen the Sands that hold the Shore.
So Stay, and Talk With Me
In the Constancy of the Moving Waters,
For I am Always There."

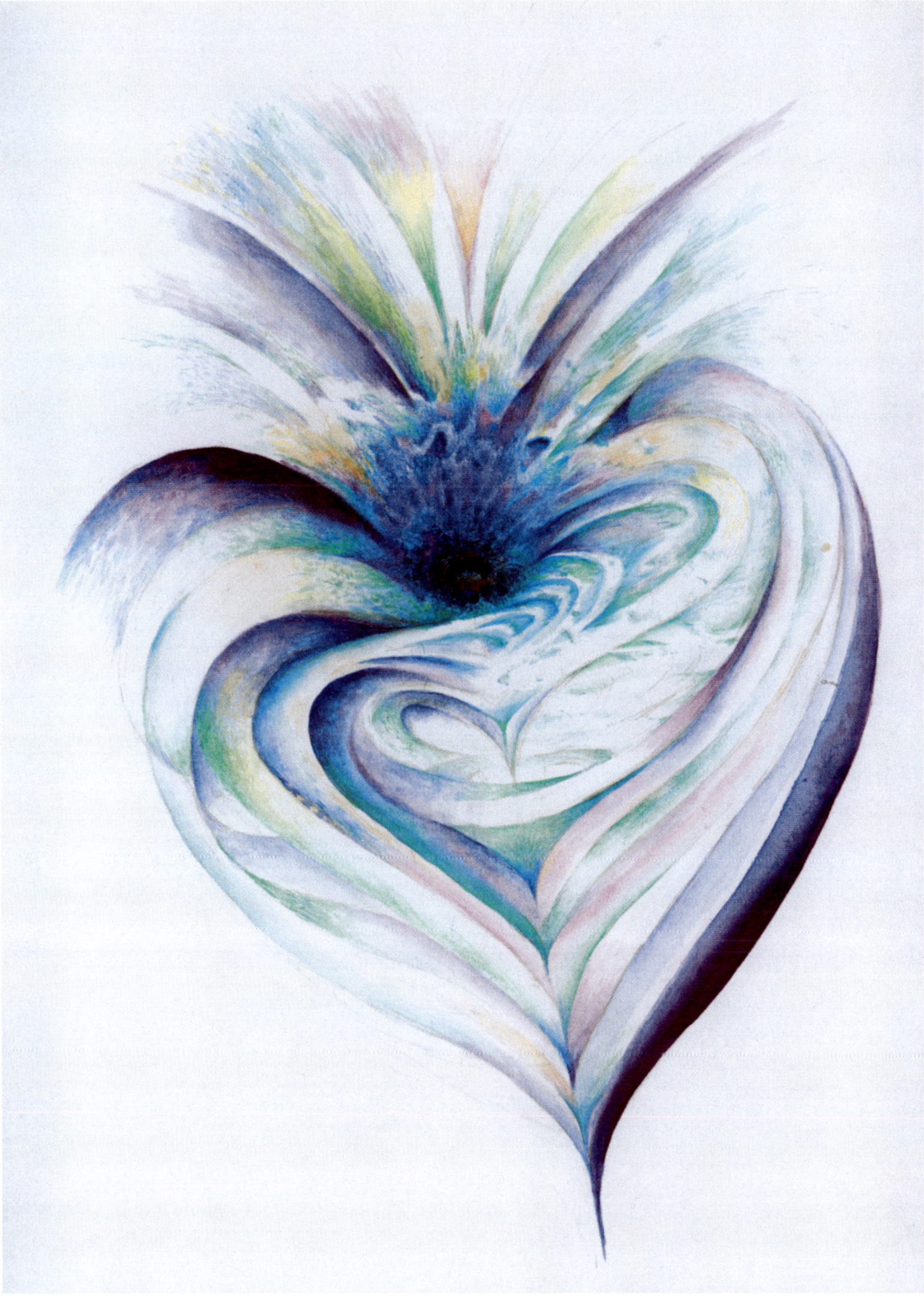

PREACHING PEBBLES.

It was a Hard and Heavy Walk Today,
For as I Disturbed those Pebbles
With the Low Tread of Tired feet
The Vibrations Resonated, and became
An inner Persistence, Pleading
"Please God, Help Me in my Confusion,
For I Know No Purpose in this Journey."
And in Response, the Air Held Its Breath,
And the Wind Lifted from the Face of the Waters,
And the Pebbles spoke through Shining Faces,
"You do not Disturb Us,
For we Too await the Will of the Tides
To Take Us on our Journey.
We Too Know Fear in the Uncertainty
Of Where we will be Taken.
We Too, are Worn away every Moment
In constant Transformation.
We Too, are place beside Unknown Companions
On an Endless Shore with no Horizon.
We Too, are Taken Where God Directs,
And We say to You,
Who Are You to Question That!"

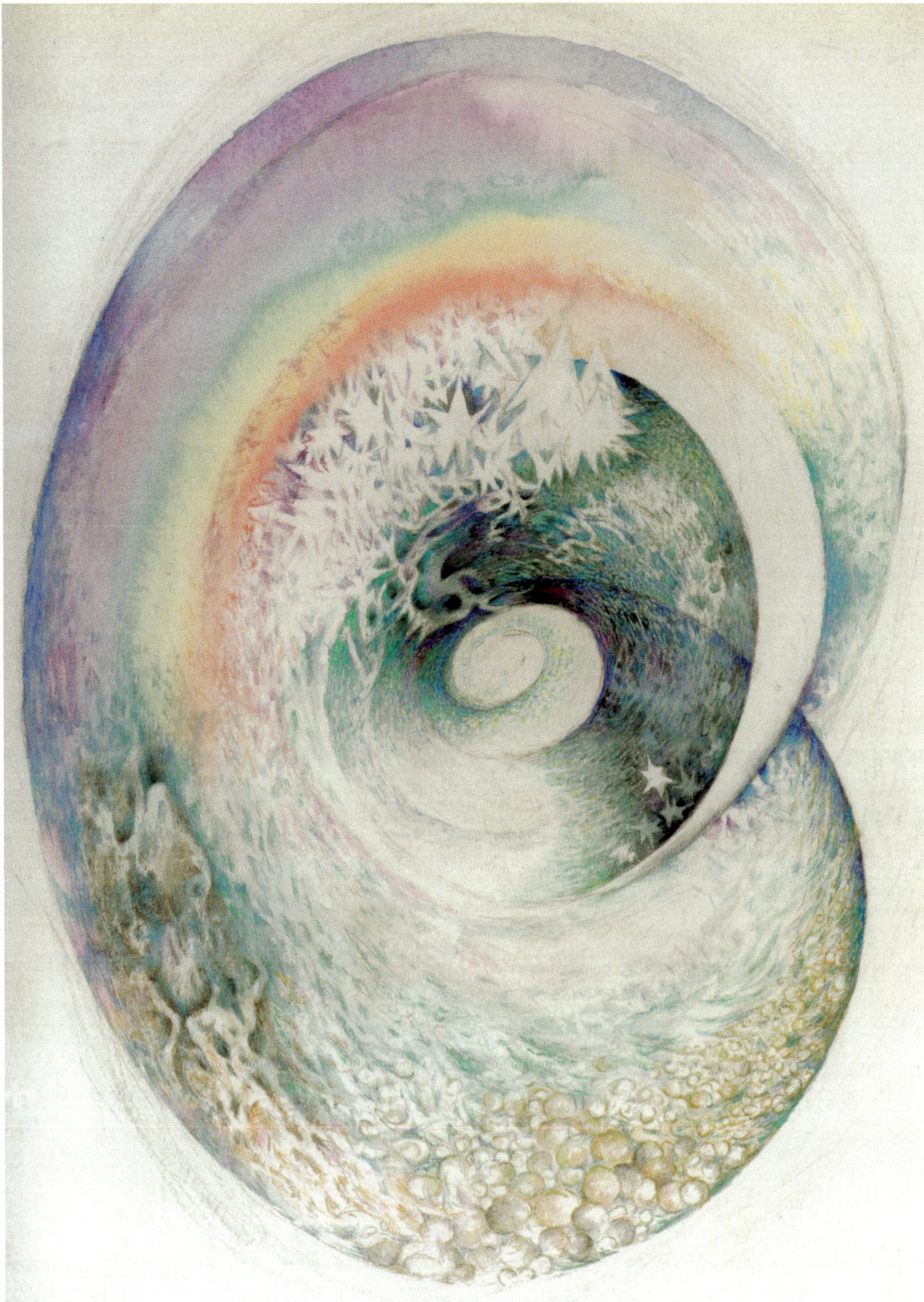

A CARGO OF COLOUR.

From the Depths of Unfathomed Waters
There appeared Vast Vessels
Floating on Waves of Light
To bring the colours of Love
Into the Darkness of the World Within.
And Held by the Breath of God
They Rise High on Immense Pillars,
Gathered in Strength by Almighty Hands
That Pull and hold, Controlling their Fury,
So they Fall, Folding Back Into Themselves
To find in the Stillness of the Depths
The Peace to Re-Create Their Shape.
And Sprawling in this Turmoil, the Vessels Tilt,
And Spill their Treasury of Colours
Onto the Face of the Waters.
And, as every Particle Vibrates,
Gyrating in the Intensity of Being,
They race in their own Lightness,
Splashing each other with Tears of Laughter
That Trickle Together as Rainbows,
Shining on the Surface of Infinity.

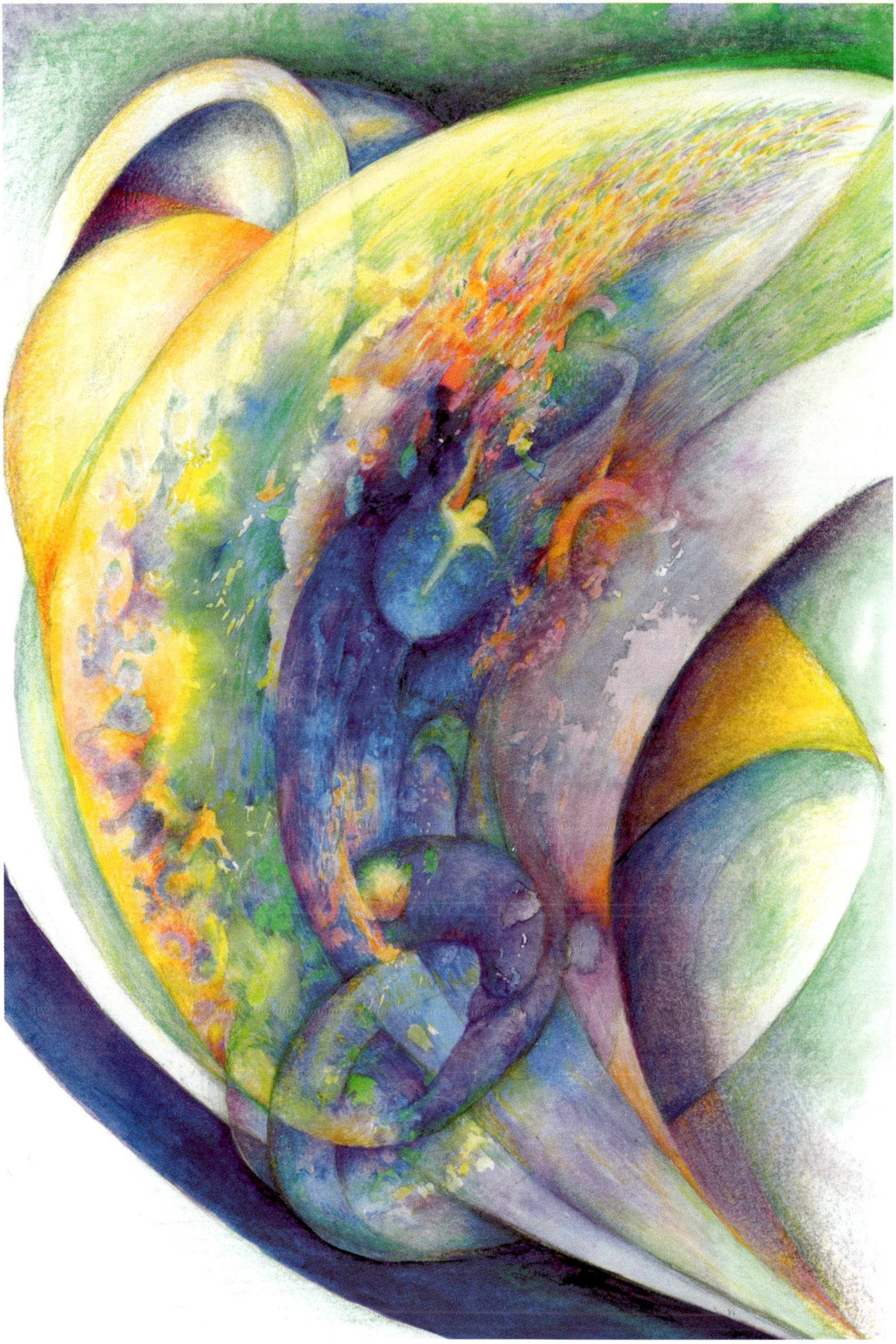

DANCING WITH DOUBT.

Sometimes it seems Empty,
Crying in a Universe of Silence.
And so Tonight I ask

If Angels Dance in the Heart of the Fire
To Kindle Light in the Darkness,
Why can't I Be There?

If Angels Smile their Thoughts
To Smooth the Turbulence of the Waters,
Why can't I Be There?

If Angels Laugh their Language
To signpost Spirals in the Sky,
Why can't I Be There?

If Angels Sing their Songs
To soothe the Hurting of the Earth,
Why can't I Be There?

And in the Night,
The Angels Smiled and Laughed
And Danced and Sang, "YOU CAN

For when you Smile and Laugh,
And Dance your Doubts,
You Sing With Us!"

THE SEASONS SPEAK.

I AM the Spreading Carpet of Creation
Woven by Wonder into a Fabric of Pattern and Light
That Hangs in the Summer Sky.

I AM the Tears of Twilight in Colour-Turning Leaves,
Surrendering in Golden Trust, not Fear,
Their Spent Strength, into the Folds of Autumn.

I AM the Resonance of the Flowing Feather, as It Frills
And Slows Its Flight into the Stillness of Winter,
Awaiting Its Uplifting on the Fresh Fingers of the Spring.

I AM the Song of the Water, Singing Itself to Sleep
As the Ice Locks Its Soul Into Silence,
To Lie in Comfort with Its Sister Earth.

But Now, I'm asked to Speak of the Agony of the Earth
Crying in Itself at the Greed of her Children,
Knowing how they Destroy their Inheritance.

I have to Talk of her Distress, as they Tear Her Apart,
And Desecrate Her Inner Sanctuaries
To Steal the Treasures, Hidden in Her Heart.

I Hear the Sigh of Steepled Grass,
Struggling to Grasp the Smile of Sunlight,
EVEN as It's Flattened by Chemical Feet.

I Listen to the Laughing Language of Life,
As Flowers Harmonise their Tones and Tunes,
EVEN as they Fade in their short Daylight.

I Touch the Supple Limbs of Toiling Roots
As they Bind Together to Hold the Shifting Soil,
EVEN as they are Chopped by Deadened Hands.

I Feel the Worm along Its Busy Passages,
Absorbing and Refining the Energy of Decay,
EVEN as It Replenishes The Body, So Diseased.

THE HURTING EARTH.

"AS WITHOUT, SO WITHIN."

And the Lord God planted a Garden Eastward in Eden, and there he put Man Whom he had Formed. And out of the Ground made the Lord to Grow every Tree that is pleasant to the Sight, and good for Food; The Tree of Life also in The midst of the Garden, and the Tree of Knowledge, of Good and Evil.

(GENESIS 2 8-9)

Let us Look at the Symbols that were given for Our Understanding..........
The Golden Thread that God made to hold the Earth on Its Course,
Is Shredding and Fraying under the strain of Man's Demands, and
Its Distortion stretches beyond Its Shape to affect All Without.
The Tree is symbolic of our Interdependence,
For the Strength of the Trunk at Its Centre
Holds together Its Extremities, in their need of Each Other.
And the Serpent uncoils around Its Trunk, seeking for Unity.
And from Within, Mother Earth Diversifies,
And flows out in Love, to embrace her Offspring.
So from the Plant Kingdom, we see the Pea swelling within Its pod.
From the kingdom of Creatures,
There lies the Larvae, laced within the Honeycomb,
And in Its Growth within the Egg, the Child stirs
To Break through Its protective Coat and find Its Feet.
The Butterfly appears, Freed by transforming Wings
To rise from Earth into the Air, in transitory Perfection.
And below the Fall of rising Tides
The Fish glides, in tune with those rhythms
Showing that in the depths of our Intuition, we Know
A need to flow in harmony with Creation.
And now, the Snail moves through the Picture,
Saying "Pause, withdraw into your Shell when you are Fearful
For within Its dark Retreat, you can talk to your Soul in comfort,
And come to know, the Duality of your Being."
And Underground , the self-replicating Worm works unseen,
Building Bridges from Decay to Renewal.
And so to the Phoenix rising from the Volcano,
A symbol of Fertility born from Destruction.
All are symbols showing Our Nature,
If only we would Open Our Eyes, and See!

And the Lord God said, Behold the Man is become as One of Us,
To know Good and Evil; And now lest he put forth his Hand
And take also from the Tree of Life, and eat and live Forever;
Therefore the Lord God sent him forth from the Garden of Eden.

(GENESIS 3 22-23)

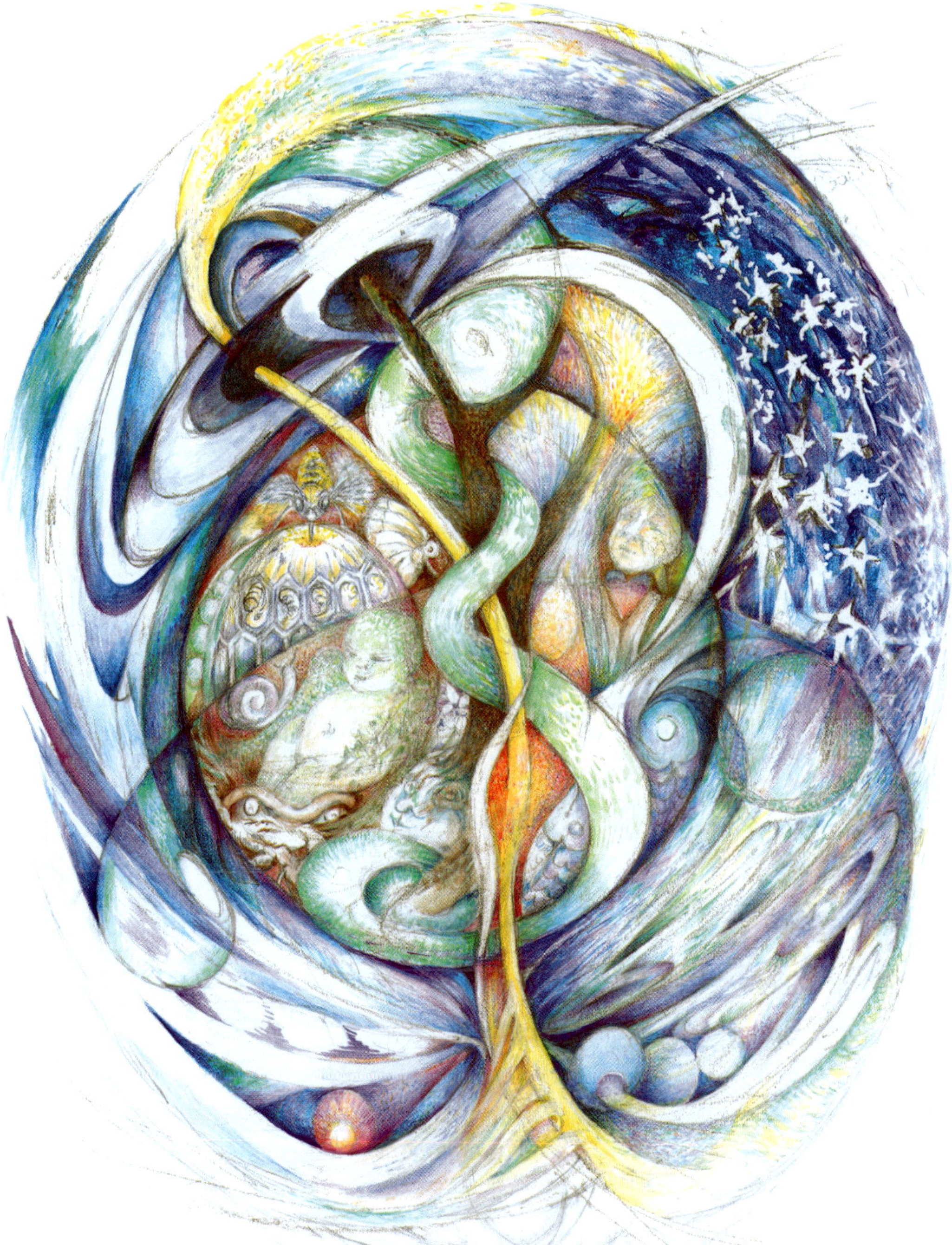

THE PERPETUAL PATTERN.

SPRING.
Long Ago in a Forgotten Time,
Begotten in the Love of God,
My Being was held in a tiny Tear
That Swelled and Came to Fullness
Shedding as dancing Rainbows, to Race
Through Space and meet with Friends
Deep in the lake of Laughter.

SUMMER.
And in the Warmth of her Huge Belly,
We Hugged Each Others Changing Shapes
And Wrapped our Colours in Curving Ripples
That Stippled Stars across her Lap
Through the Gaze of a Smiling Sun.

AUTUMN.
But there could be no Perpetual Playtime,
Our Colours Fell and Faded
As through the Grey Mists of Autumns Ageing
The Sun Sucked in its Smile
And Drew Me through to Share its Lightness
Free to Float on Fleecy Thermals
Through Airy Halls of Cloistered Clouds,
And see the Unravelling of Infinity
Around, Above and Below Me.

WINTER.
Then Came the Turning of the Season,
The Sun Scowled, Frowning thro' Crypted Clouds
And I Sank, Trapped in their Blackness
As Winter Splintered their Hearts
And Cut them to Frosted Fragments.
The Clouds Wept the Cruelty of their Shredding,
And Shed their Tears of Icy Spears
To Pierce the Shivering Earth.

All was Silent, All was Still, Nothing Spoke,
As I Lay There shining my Sadness to the Sky
From Where I had Fallen, Yet Knowing,
That though Captured in this Crystal Cloak
The Time of Release would Come
In the Melting Movement of the Spring,
And I would Be Free to Run Again
Back to the Lake of Laughter.

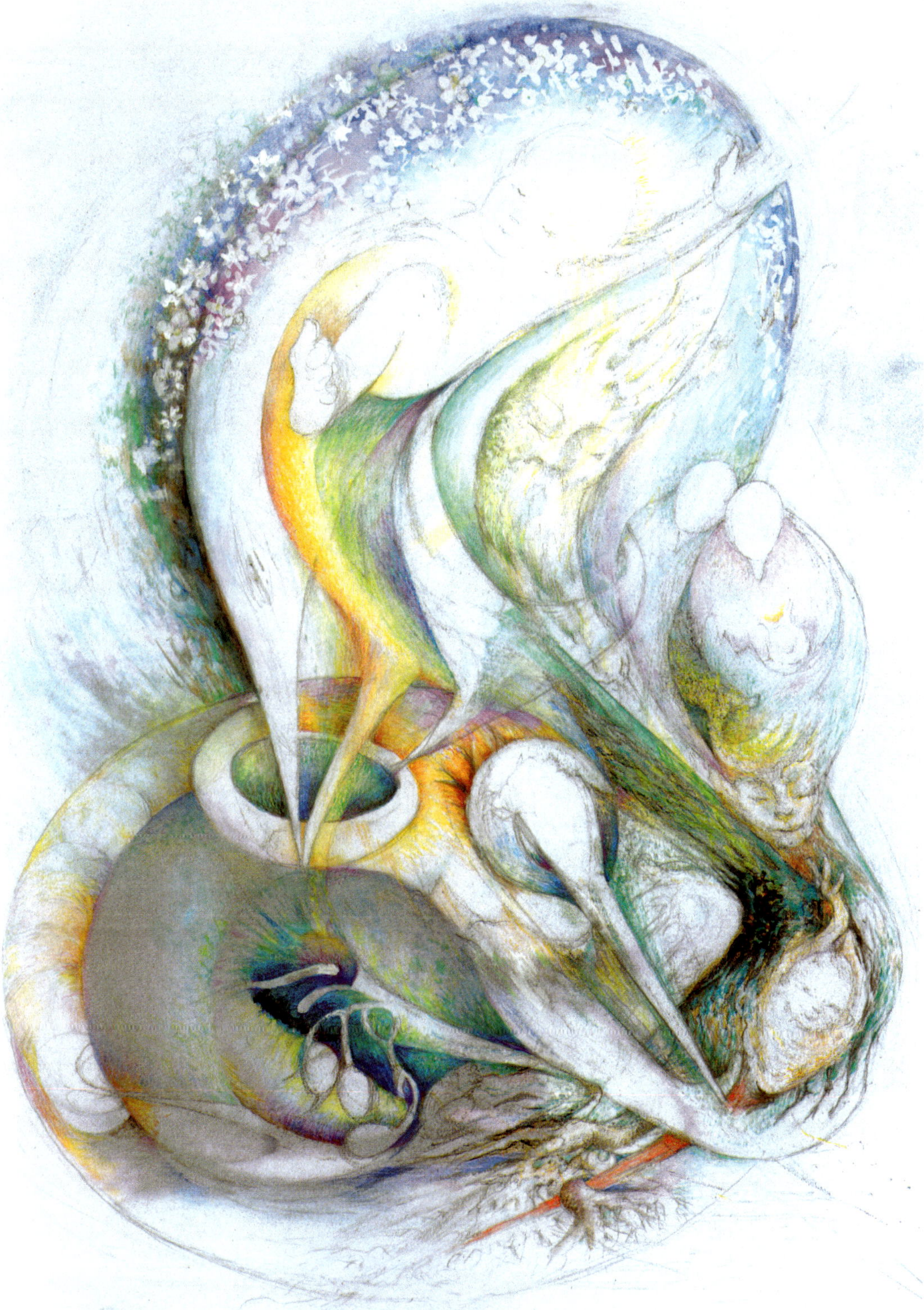

SISTER SEASONS.

SUMMER. "WE REAP WHAT WE SOW."
A Universal Design governs All that Manifests,
But All that Manifests is Unique.
In Trepidation we Take Our Power into our Being
To Flower in the Garden of synchronised Creation,
For as we expand out to Be in touch with Others,
We also contract in, to Be in touch with Our Self.
As the Nectar of the Flower is Essential
for the Bee to Serve Its Purpose
So the visiting Bee is Essential to Serve the Seeding of the Plant.
So the generosity of the Summer Is a Time of Trust
To Open Up, and Engage in Cosmic Contracts
Between the eager sprouting steps of Spring,
And the stiffening gait of Autumn's ageing.
For Summer Binds them both Together,
That in the Garden God Designed
Our Being can Flower in Its Given Time.

AUTUMN. "WE DISINTEGRATE TO INTEGRATE".
The Waters withdraw, bleeding dry the Flesh of blushing Fruits.
Summer disintegrates into Itself to feed her dormant Seeds,
And Gaia gathers them to the comfort of her Breast
To Rest and Awaken refreshed from their winter sleep.
The Fire without Light to fuel Its Flame
Cast Off Its Colours as Glowing Embers,
Whose smouldering Remains die down,
To Scatter browned Ashes across the Ground.
And the Air Takes Breath as foaming Winds
That scour and clear those tawdry Leaves,
Hanging so tired on the limbs of Trees
And from this Moulting, their Structure once concealed
Stand stark and Stripped revealing their intricate Sculpture.

"REGENERATION."
Autumn is a time of Contemplation,
For Seeing the Coming Confinement
Not as a Punishment, but a time of Expectation.
As Compressed by the cold Judgement of Winter
We will be squeezed between Its heavy Hands
To arise renewed into the Spring,
And stride with the Sun on Its purposeful Path,
Finding Fulfilment in the Strength of the Summer,
Before Autumn returns to reclaim us again.

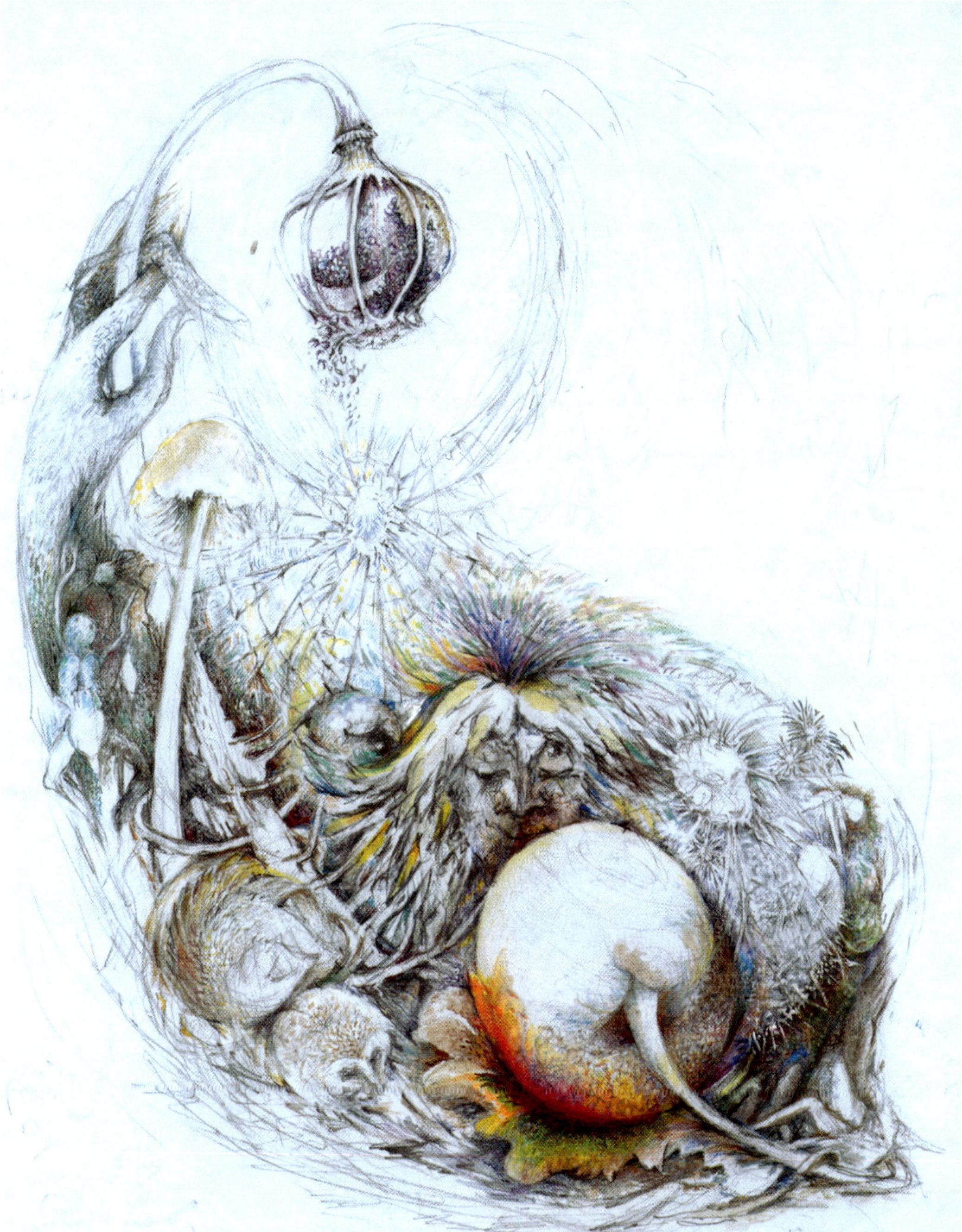

THAT LEAF CALLED LUCIFER.

As Autumn turns Its tired Back,
And creeps under the chill coat of Winter
There, that last Leaf resisted on the Twig,
Insisting in Its Conceit, "Don't Shed me yet,
For I Am the Energy that sustains you
By Transforming the light from above.
And only when I Am ready to Depart,
Will I change the colour of My clothes,
And Parade proudly down to Earth
In a solitary show of Glory."
The Tree trembled with a Mother's Fear
At the defiance of her arrogant Son,
As the Twig on which It had clung too long,
Begged to be relieved of its Burden.
The parent Branch shook Itself in disbelief
At this Betrayal of the Timeless Pattern,
And breathed Its Distress into the Sap.
And in the Break Down of Law and Order,
The Sap in confusion, retreated to the Roots
To seek for a resolution of the Discord.
And from their seat deep in the Ground,
The Roots said, "We too have profound concern
In the Treason of That Leaf, for It affects us All.
So let us call on the Collective Wisdom of our Core
To give Judgement in Its central Court." And There
The Core consulted All Its Constituents
Before pronouncing Its final Sentence.
"Your Down fall Is inevitable.
You are condemned in your contempt
For the Structure of the Seasons.
Your sisters now shroud the Ground,
And you should be There with them
Sharing the grief of their Decay.
For you have Had Your Given Time,
To turn, and Flirt your coloured Face.
Know now, that only God Dictates
The length of the Journey you make."
And the Twig now freed from that long held Grip,
Watched with relief as That sullen Leaf,
Still sulky Green, shrugged Its withered Shoulders
And slipped tight lipped to the Ground.

A TIME TO REST.

In these troubled Times of Transition,
Lay down your Body
And give It Rest,
For Its strength is needed
To Carry your Soul.
  Lay down your Head,
  And surrender your Thoughts
  To the amazing Message
  That your Soul is giving.
Let your Insight
Give you the Light that you need,
Not Hindsight, or Foresight,
For they are only Shadows
That Disappear into the Darkness of Existence.
  Let your Intuition
  Give you the Guidance that you need,
  And Look Not to Others for Knowledge,
  For That Wisdom talks from Within.
Let your Integrity
Give you the Certainty of Your Truth
For though Others speak their Truths,
They are but Echoes of the Inner Voice
Of your Own Soul Speaking,
Beseeching You to Listen,
Inside Out, Outside In, and take delight
In Who You Are!

"MY WORST HABIT IS I GET SO TIRED OF WINTER I BECOME A TORTURE TO THOSE I'M WITH." (RUMI,)

But Rumi, Winter is the Season of Rest.
A Time to Close our Eyes, and Reflect Inside
On the Dormant Truths we saw
As we passed through Its Sister Seasons.
And in the Darkness, lighten on those tiny Gems
That were Hidden in their Garments....................
The exuberant Flirting of the Bare-Legged Spring,
Giving Witness to the Certainty of Resurrection.
The Billowing Smile of Full-Skirted Summer,
Giving Witness to the Ecstasy of Fulfillment,
And in the Ragged Trappings of the Autumn,
We Witness the Agony of the Crucifixion.
But in the Exposure of Finery Torn Away,
We have No Need to Steal the Clothes of Others,
Rather, in our Nakedness curl Inside,
And Know that the Warmth that Is Within,
Nurtures the Seed of Our Renewal.

SIGNS OF WINTER.

"AS ABOVE, SO BELOW."

When the Light
Drains Out,
It leaves us in the Dark.
When the warmth
Drains Out,
It leaves us in the Cold.
When the Laughter
Drains out,
It leaves us in Despair.
When the Love
Drains Out,
It leaves us in Emptiness.

In this Time of separation from our Source above,
God sends his Love through Signs and Symbols,
But even as we seek their True Translation,
We deny the verification offered by our Soul.
For it is a Language that Unites, not Separates,
And in the Open Figure Eight, the Spirit waits
To create a Bridge from Earth to sky.
The Triangles are a Trinity of Lines,
That tell of the Three Aspects of Oneness.
For as their Feet are firmly founded in the Ground,
So their Arms reach up through the open Air,
Sharing their need to come Together,
And touch in Heaven, as Hands in Prayer.
The Dual Moons' above, that seemed in opposition,
Now curve inwards seeking reunion with each other.
Whilst Those beneath, reach to their central Core
To Hold once more, the Pot of Knowledge
Gathered from the Passing Year.
And as we peer below Its Rim
To evaluate what we see within,
The Reflecting Star gives Insight
Beyond the greed of Burdened Fear,
Pointing Its Fingers of icy light, to the Crystals
That fuel the Flame of Love.
And rising from purified Pools within,
The Dove holds open the Arch of Heaven,
That the Soul may seek from the Star above
Guidance through Its secret Veils
Into the Presence of Its Creator.

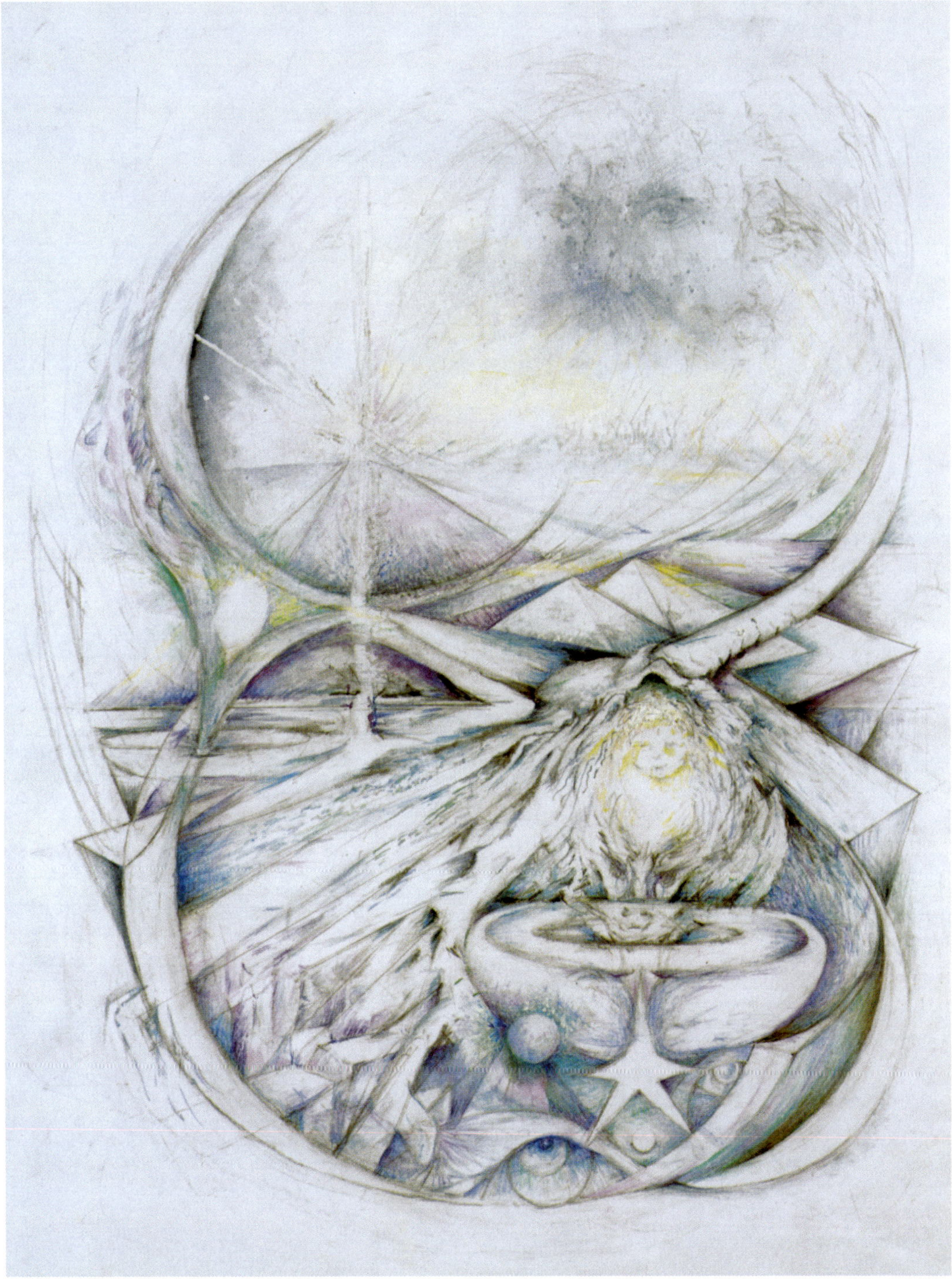

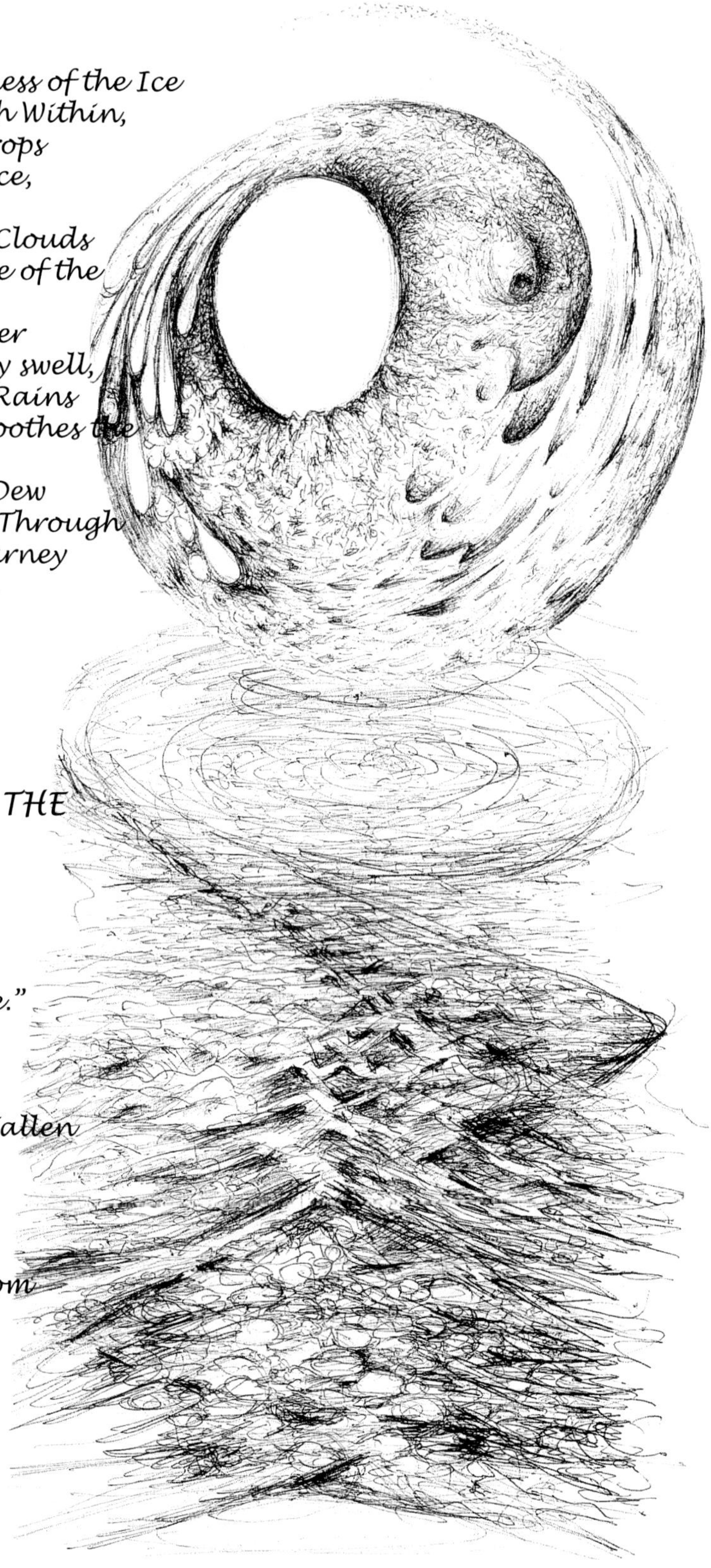

LIQUIDITY!

From the cold smoothness of the Ice
That carries Its warmth Within,
To the Chrystal Raindrops
That in their Transience,
Rise as Vapour
To form insubstantial Clouds
Surging across the Face of the
Heavens.
Until, gathered together
In their Heaviness, they swell,
And fall again as the Rains
Whose healing touch soothes the
Earth,
Leaving Diamonds of Dew
To mark their Passing Through
On their spiralling Journey
Back into the Heavens.

THE SEA SPEAKS TO THE RIVER.

"IN this Flood-Time
I'm Full to the Brim,
So Go Away, Go Back
From whence you Came."
And the River Cried,
With swollen Eyes,
"How can that Be ?"
For my Substance has Fallen
From the Clouds.
How can I Return
Without the Fire
To Warm my Essence,
And give me the Freedom
To Ascend again
From whence I Came".

DUALITY AND DOUBT.

For too long, we have created God in our Image,
And only when we can accept Our Divinity
With a Certainty, that stands beyond Fear,
Then we can revere the need of God
To show Himself in us. For in our Entity,
We ARE the Elements of Duality!
We are the whispering Waters of the Rain,
Of the Stream, the Ocean, and the Flood
Of Movement and of Stillness.
Of Nurture and of Drowning,
For that IS our Duality!
We are the Transparency of the Air,
Of the Breeze, the Wind and the Hurricane,
Whose Breath gives Life to Thought and Feeling.
To rise in Trust on unknown Thermals, or remain
In the Damp Distrust of drowning Clouds.
For that IS our Duality!
We are, the procreating Earth,
That Grounds us in compassionate Arms,
Even as It releases us from her Hold.
And as Guardians of her generous Gifts,
We can cherish, and respect her Sacrifice, or,
As Children still, demand more than she can Give.
For that IS our Duality!
We are the eternal Fire of the Universe,
That can consume in uncontrolled Rage,
Or can Be the silent Candle Flame
Giving comfort in Its steady Gaze.
For that IS our Duality!
But most Essential to our Being,
Is our return to Unity,
Through the cordless Ether of the unknown,
The invisible Threading that weaves together
All Elements Into Itself.
So let us not Be Selfish, but rather, Self-Full,
In response to our Duality.

ME AND MY IMAGE.

I See Those Shapes
Lying Flat
Across the Blankness
Of the Sky,
And ask,
"Does that have to Be Me?"
For the World is Full
Of Shedding Tears,
And in the Forming Puddle
I Watch the Drop
Disform The Image,
And ask,
"Is That Me?"

At the Edges of Today
Tomorrow is already There,
Reflecting the Tears of Yesterday
As a Blink in the Eye of Sadness.
So Today on this silent Shore,
I Sent my Soul Into the Sea
To Search for Where I Am.

And as It Sank, I Heard It Crying,
Crucified by the Sharp-Toothed Tides.
And It Returned on Frayed Fingers
To Touch my Shell and say,
"Please Come With Me
For I Cannot Walk on the Water
Without You There, with Me."

And I Curled Up Inside,
And replied, "If Only I Could Come Today,
But Yesterday we didn't keep Company,
Perhaps Tomorrow?"
Though I Knew,
That Tomorrow
Needed to Be Today!"

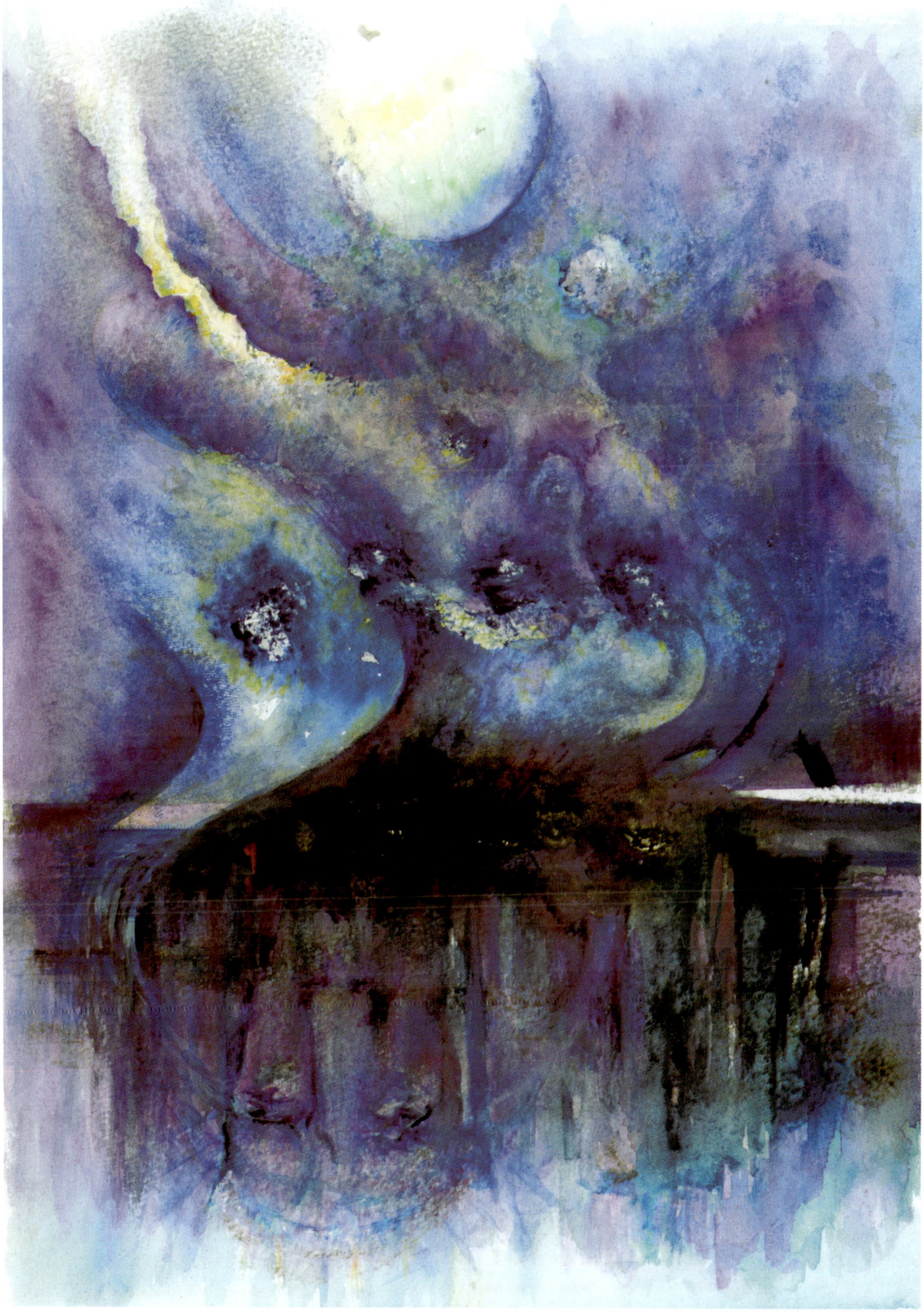

A TWILIGHT DAY.

This was a Twilight Day.
As the Sun struggled
To Escape the Clothing Clouds,
It was torn into Grey Edged Strips.
For the Clouds, so filled with Water
Could no longer contain Themselves
And Spilled their exhausted Strength
As huge Tears, dropping silently
To pass their Hurt to Mother Earth.
        But as we looked out to Sea,
        It remained Untouched
        By the heavy handed Rain.
        Everywhere seemed saturated Grey,
        The Sky Hung in heavy Folds
        Scowling Its Greyness at us.
The Sea Swelled in Its Fury
And threw Itself Enraged
Along the grey gravelled Shore.
The Land limped in hazy Layers
Along the Horizon of the Heavens,
A Sinking Container
That God had made to hold the Seas,
Even as they Ate into Its Edges.
        It gave a grey glimpse
        Of where we Are in Transformation,
        Of knowing Too, that our Inner Ocean
        Is Gnawing at our Edges
        To Free our Spirits
        From the Boundaries of the Mind,
So Thank you, for the Greyness of Today.

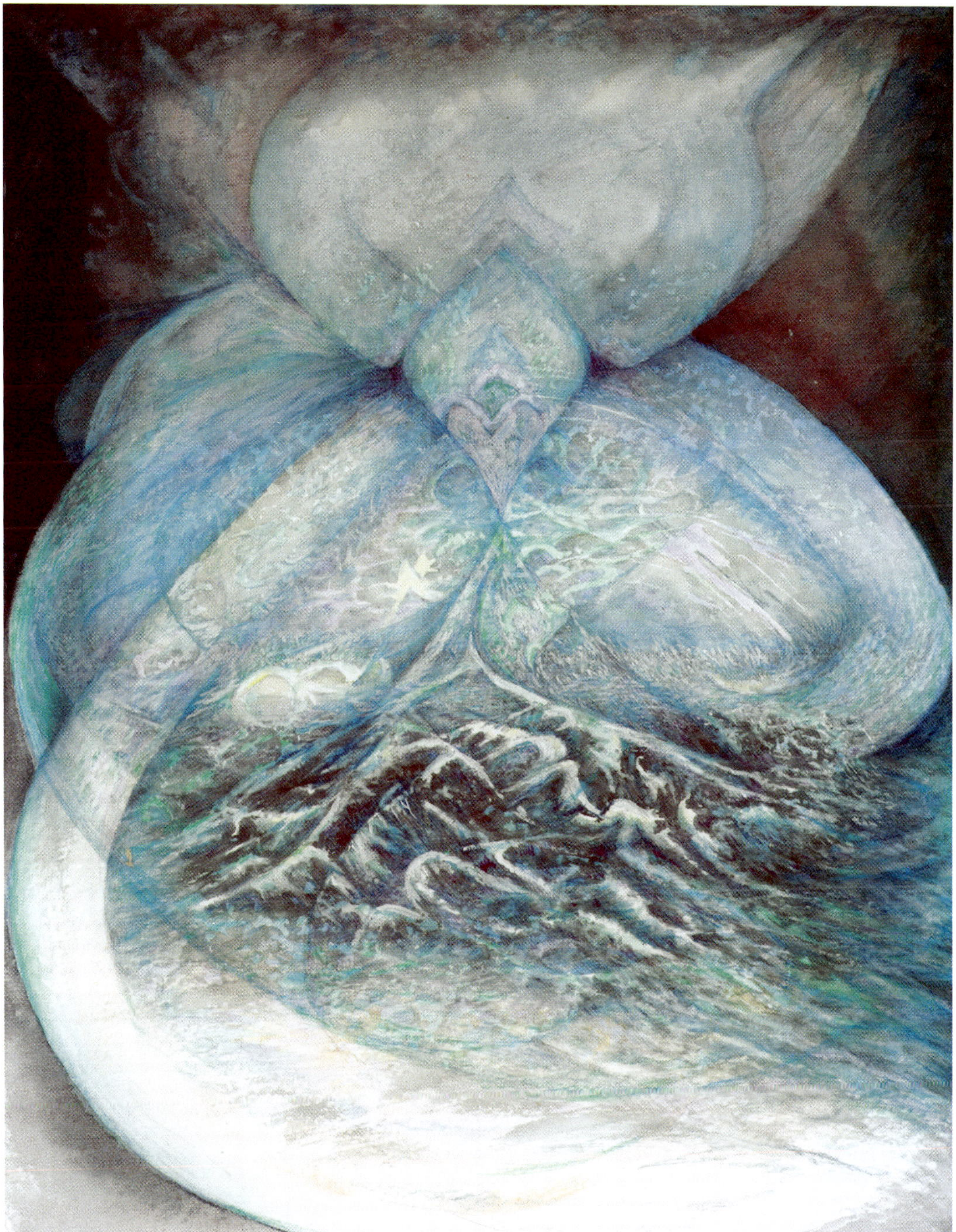

GREY ENERGY.

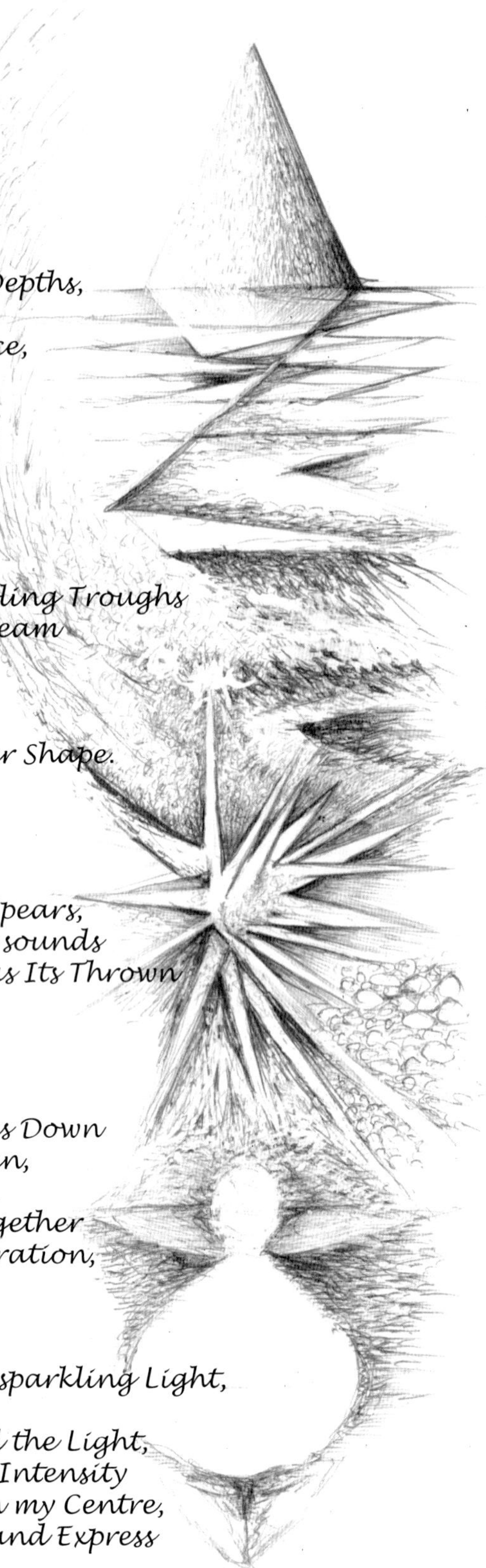

GREY is the Balance.....
It's about the Infinity of Tone
Between Light and Darkness.
I Love Grey, for It Is All Tones
Between Black and White
Without the Distraction of Colour.
Though I struggle in my own Tonal Depths,
I Know that
Ice is a Grey-Green White Translucence,
Its silent Surface never Still,
For It Reflects All that moves Above It.
But the movement Within is Unseen,
Until It Transforms
And Melts to Water again,
What does That say to Me?

And in the exuberant energy of tumbling Troughs
That Erupt from the Surface of the Stream
And throw up silky Threads of Foam
To Catch the Colours from the Sky,
Even as they Fall into themselves
They Translate to the Tones of another Shape.
What does That say to Me?

And through
The Titanic Crash of Warrior Waves,
That smash each other to splintered Spears,
In smothered Shrouds of Foam, there sounds
The Grey-green of Re-Birthing, even as Its Thrown
To Die on a stony Shore.
What does That say to Me?

And in the Night
When the Warmth of the Moon reaches Down
To Lay across the coldness of the Ocean,
The Horizon softens Into a grey Halo,
Gathering the Heavens and Earth Together
In a forever Hug, that knows No Separation,
What does That say to Me?

And Now, I Say,
"That on a Diamond Path Forged by sparkling Light,
I become transparent in my Greyness,
For on Either Side, I see the Dark and the Light,
And Know that I can't Survive in the Intensity
Of Their Extremes, but need to Stay In my Centre,
For only There can I Absorb, Reflect, and Express
The Whole Tonality of "Being!"

THE MIRROR IN THE SEA.

And God said,
Come sit with Me by the Sea
That you may know My Ways.
For My Ways are Mirrored in its Rhythms
That are given for you to Attune to,
And bring you back to Me.

And in the clarity of that Dimension,
We Became the Waves, strong Warriors
That Strode the shining Surface,
Humped with brown steeled Backs
As they raced towards the Beach.

We Became their Pause of Pace,
Waiting on the Crest of an Indrawn Breath,
Poised for the Command to Charge
Across the guarding Sand
And Penetrating the softness of Its Belly
To undermine the defenceless Land.

But that bold dash from the Horizon Line
Had exhausted our United Force,
As our plunging Horses broke their Legs
Our Expended Energy was cut to Shreds,
And we Scattered far in Disarray,
Throwing away our tattered Cloaks
In Surrender on the forgiving Shore.

And laid to Rest in the shifting Shingle
Our tingling Remains were Turned,
And our Worn Out Intensity transformed
Into a Contrary Energy
We Became Fingers of Foam,
Creeping in to Explore the Shore,
And search for Its Vulnerability,
For we knew, by Looking in the Mirror,
Humility, not Fury, was the way to Victory.

THE MOON SMILED.

As the Moon Floated through
The Filtering Fingers of the Dawn,
It called from the Shadows,
"Go down to the Sea
And Hear the Sounds I Create,
And See the Vision of Wonder
That I unfold before your Eyes."
But Today seemed Unfocused,
For I wasn't prepared to Listen
And closed my Eyes to the Truth
That in the Depths of the Eyes
We are given sight of the Inner Ocean.
So I shed Tears to distort the Message
Carried in those Waters, and sought instead
To Share the Clarity of your Sight.
　　If only I had the Insight,
　　And the Courage to Listen
　　As the Tide demanded,
"Hear what I Be, Look at Me and See
That in the constant changes of Shape I make,
IS the clarity of Vision that you seek.
For my Energies too, Flow In and Out
In Movement with the Moon;
Showing you the Truth of Transformation,
For in the Breathing of the Universe,
We Share the Same Breath.
　　So look not to your Friend for Clarity,
　　But rather Look to Me!
　　For the Clouds that you see in her Eyes
　　Are Your Clouds, that veil you from each Other.
What Blinds you are Your Own Fears,
And the Pain that you feel in the Drying Tears
Is that of the Tide turning in Renewal.
So Open Your Eyes to Your Friend
In loving Acceptance of her Truth,
And know with what Joy that Friend
Will enter Into Your Openness;
For this Is the Gift you were given to Share."
And the Moon Smiled!

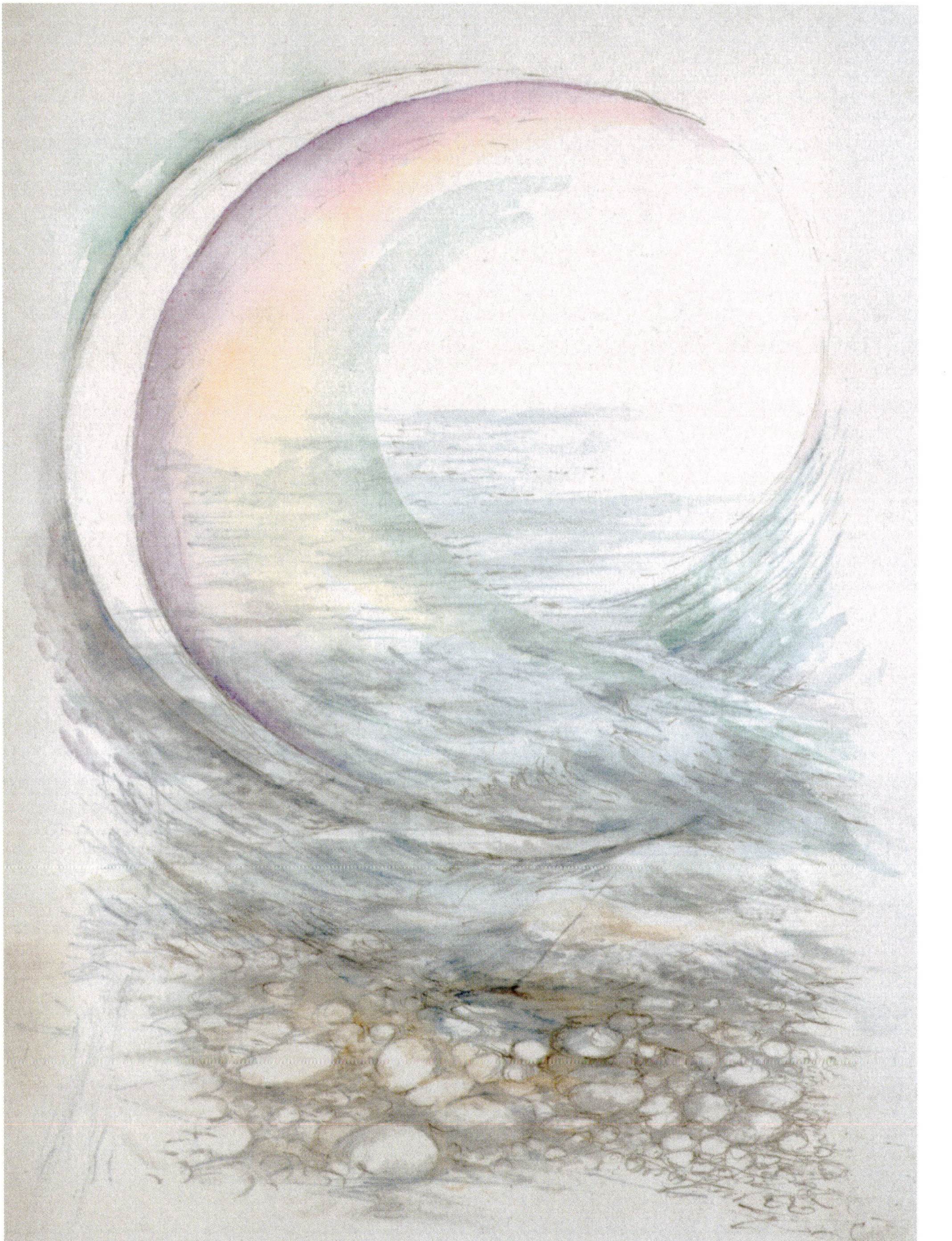

THE INNER SEA.

In the Speechless sharing of our Souls,
The Depths fill up in Lightness
As "The Mystery" was Mirrored in your Eyes,
I was drawn into that Forward Flow
As you took Me through the turning Tides,
Into that Ocean of Inner Calm.
How I wanted to Anchor in Its Stillness,
But Its Centre was the Starting Spiral
Born from the ceaseless rhythm of the Seas.
And the waves came to reclaim Me,
To take me back to the Unreality
Of this surrealistic Shore
Where Mind and Spirit
Were laid out Side by Side,
Waiting for the Turning Tide
To draw them back Together.

And as the Tide turned softly
Beneath the Skirt of the Sea,
It creased Its surface
Into shimmering Scales of Light.
A slow Dance of Sequins
That scattering along the Shore,
Took us with the into Oneness.
For even as we watched
Those tiny Streams scurrying back
Through the Skin of sloping Sand,
They were greeted by a Sisterhood of Waves
Singing, "We are Here to carry you back Home!"

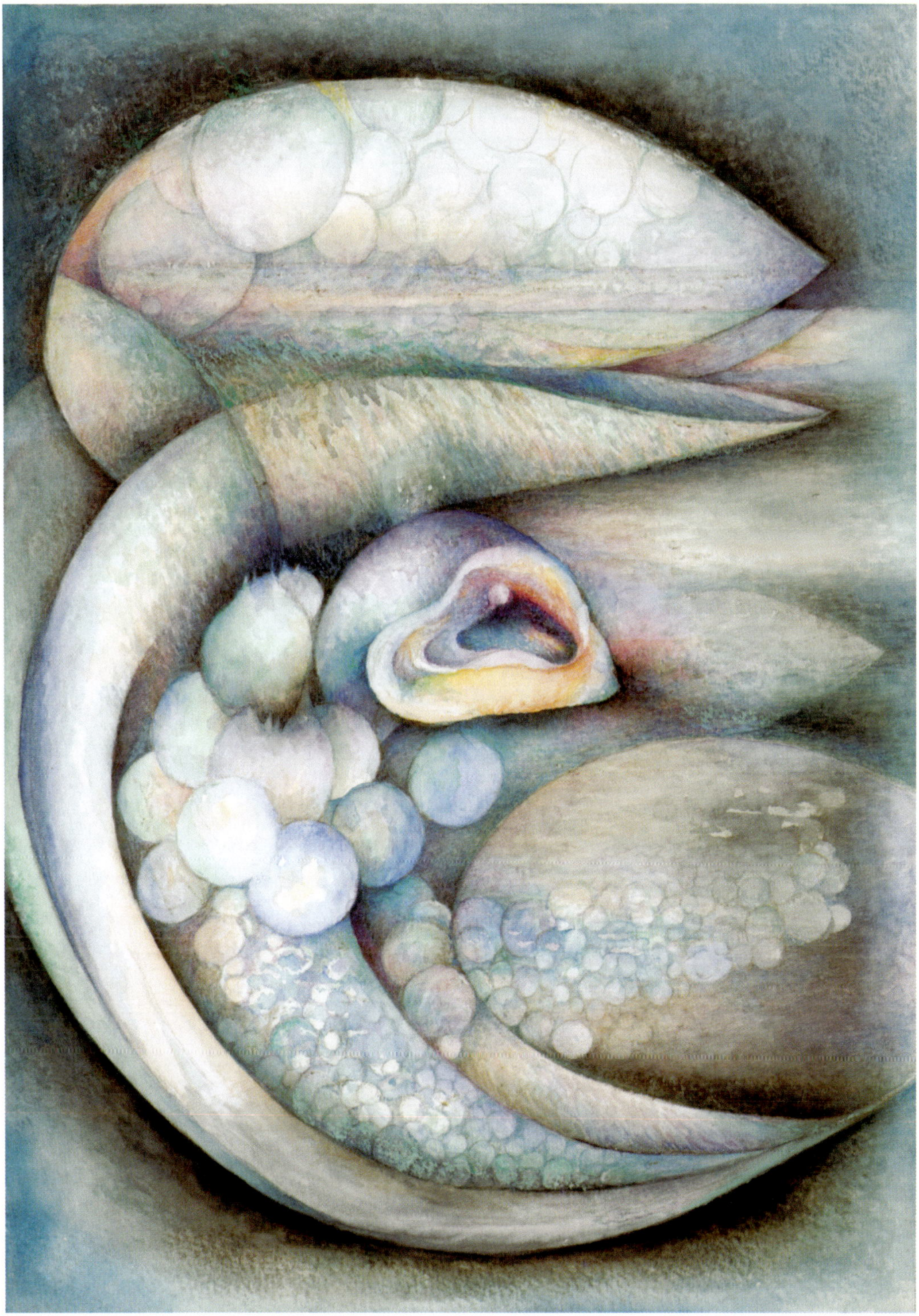

COMMUNING WITH THE SEA>

In Anticipation
The Morning held Its Breath
As the Day turned back Into Itself
To soothe the Heat of the outstretched Sun.
As we came together to walk the Shore,
We entered the soft Arms of the Afternoon,
And Bared our Feet to receive the Baptism
From the Fringe of Running Waters
That drew us into their Folds.
And in Confirmation we stood Transfixed,
As translucent Waves surging in Sunlight
Brought shining Strands of Seaweed
As an Offering at our Feet,
Before snatching It back into Its vast Playground,
Where we would not follow, for fear
That in the rough games it played,
We would be swallowed into Its Emptiness..
So we withdrew on shimmering Feet,
To sit in Communion on the shingle Beach,
And open ourselves to the Sea and the Sky
And glimpse through their dividing Line
Those invisible threads that bind them forever
Unsevered by the Hands of Time.
And in the Words of Its Liquid Prayers,
We heard the Sea sighing Its relief
In the completion of Its priestly role.
And disrobing Its Cloak in the Evening Light,
It cast the Surplice from Its Shoulders
And tore the white Ruffs from Its Throat
Before withdrawing to Its Horizon,
To find renewal in Its safe Retreat.
There was such a sense of Ordination,
In the affirmation that the Day had given.
How sad it was to Return,
And find a Parking Ticket!

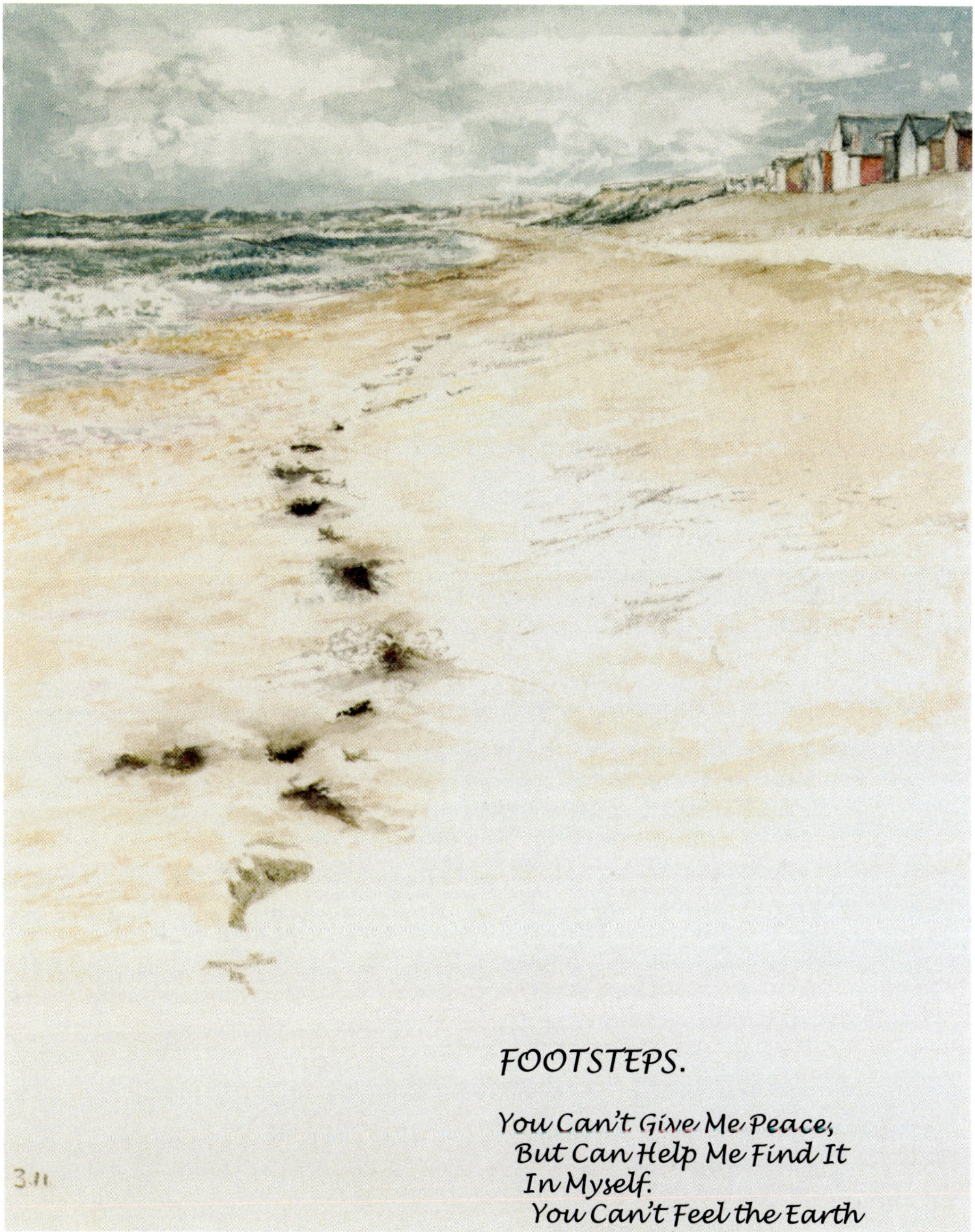

FOOTSTEPS.

You Can't Give Me Peace,
But Can Help Me Find It
In Myself.
You Can't Feel the Earth
Between My Toes,
But You Can Cover Them
In Your Warmth.
You Can't Walk For Me,
But With Me.
For My Footsteps
Are My Own,
And Make Their Own Mark.

THE DEAF CONGREGATION.

As the Waters Kissed the Shore farewell
Before Departing to their Depths
They left the Gift of a Solitary Stone
Standing on the Strands of Sand.
And tho' beyond the Waters Reach,
The Huddled Stones that lay all Heaped
In Pyre-Like Piles along the Beach,
Felt the relentless Tug of the Turning Tides
And Stirred to stare with Empty Eyes
At this Stranger, that they recognised.
And from their Shrouds of Stagnant Sleep
In fear they cried through Grated Teeth
"From Where did You Materialise,
Why Wake us with your Shining Eyes?"
And gazing up to the Veiling Sky,
The Stone spoke sadly in Reply,
"I am Pledged to Free You from this Place
But my Stay is short at the Water's Edge,
For I have travelled Far to Embrace You
Across the Endless Oceans of Time
That you may Touch Into Its Knowing
By Flowing With Me Into the Unknown
In Trust, that All will be Made Known.
For In our Movement Is our Creation,
And Re-Creation Into Being,
For Being Is Re-creation In Infinite Creation."
But in the density of that Darkness, the Words Blurred,
Their Intensity Untuned, Unheard and Unlamented,
Fragmented, and Reformed as mighty Waves of Light
That raced back to Their Source.
And all along that Barren beach,
Those Stones sank back to Sterile Sleep,
And Never saw That Stone Depart,
Crying the hurt of Its Broken Heart

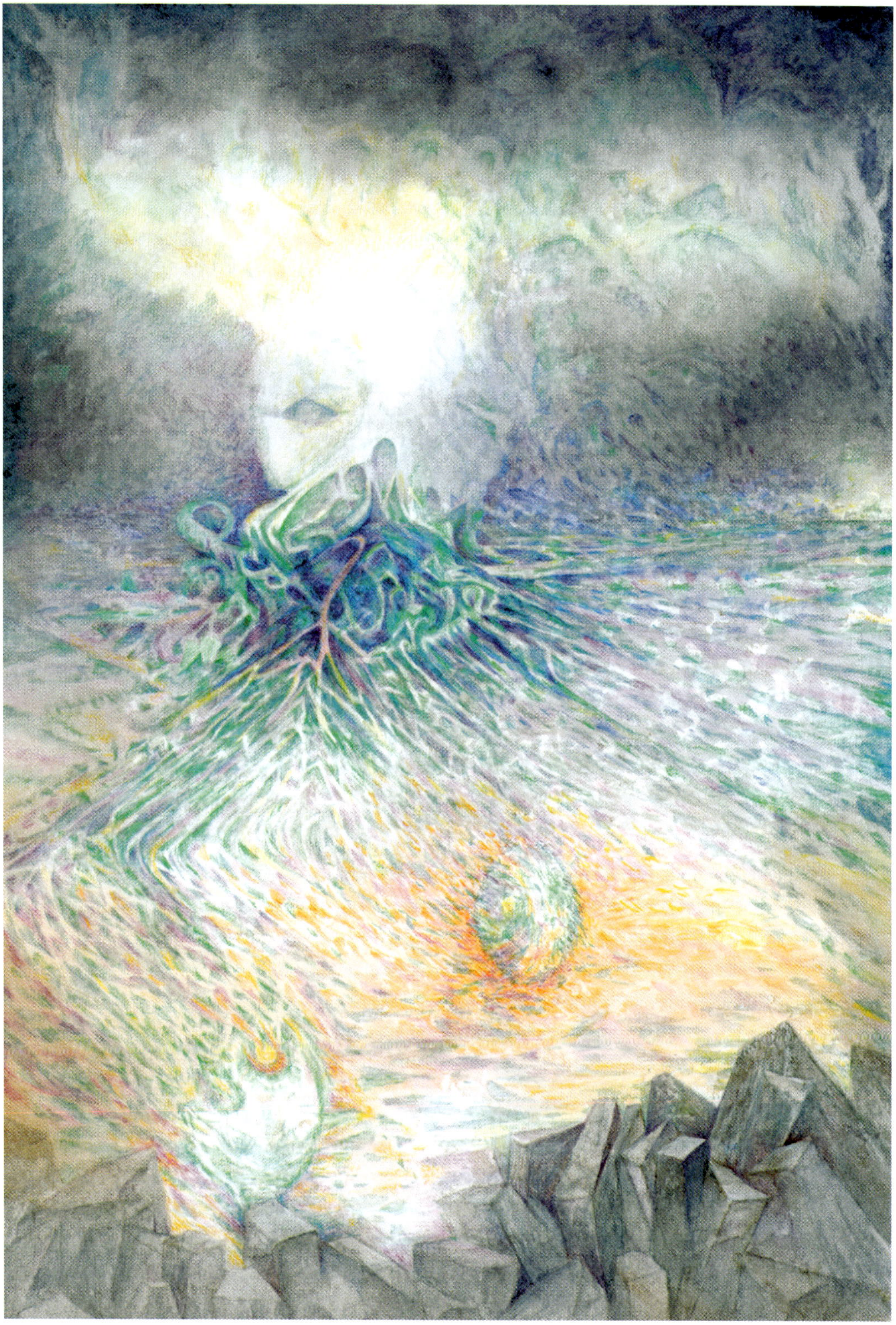

THE CALL OF THE SHORE.

The Shore is where we have been Called
Into the Allness of the Universe.
To accept, without needing to Understand,
Our Part in Its Pattern
For you were there to share
That Hugeness of Breath,
To Breath Into Becoming.
As the Diamond folds Back
Into the forms from which it came,
To become again the Two Triangles
United in their Wholeness, but Separate,
How can that Be?

I cry in my Transformation
As I turn Into Myself,
My diamond Face distorted
By the streaming Tears
That run from the Shore
Taking me with them
Through the curtained tunnel
Of the Shroud, and into the Light
That hides behind the Clouds.

For I was part of Its meaning
As It became a wider Perception;
For the Line of the Horizon
Became invisioned All Around,
Above, Below and Beyond my Vision,
Into the realms of Mystery.

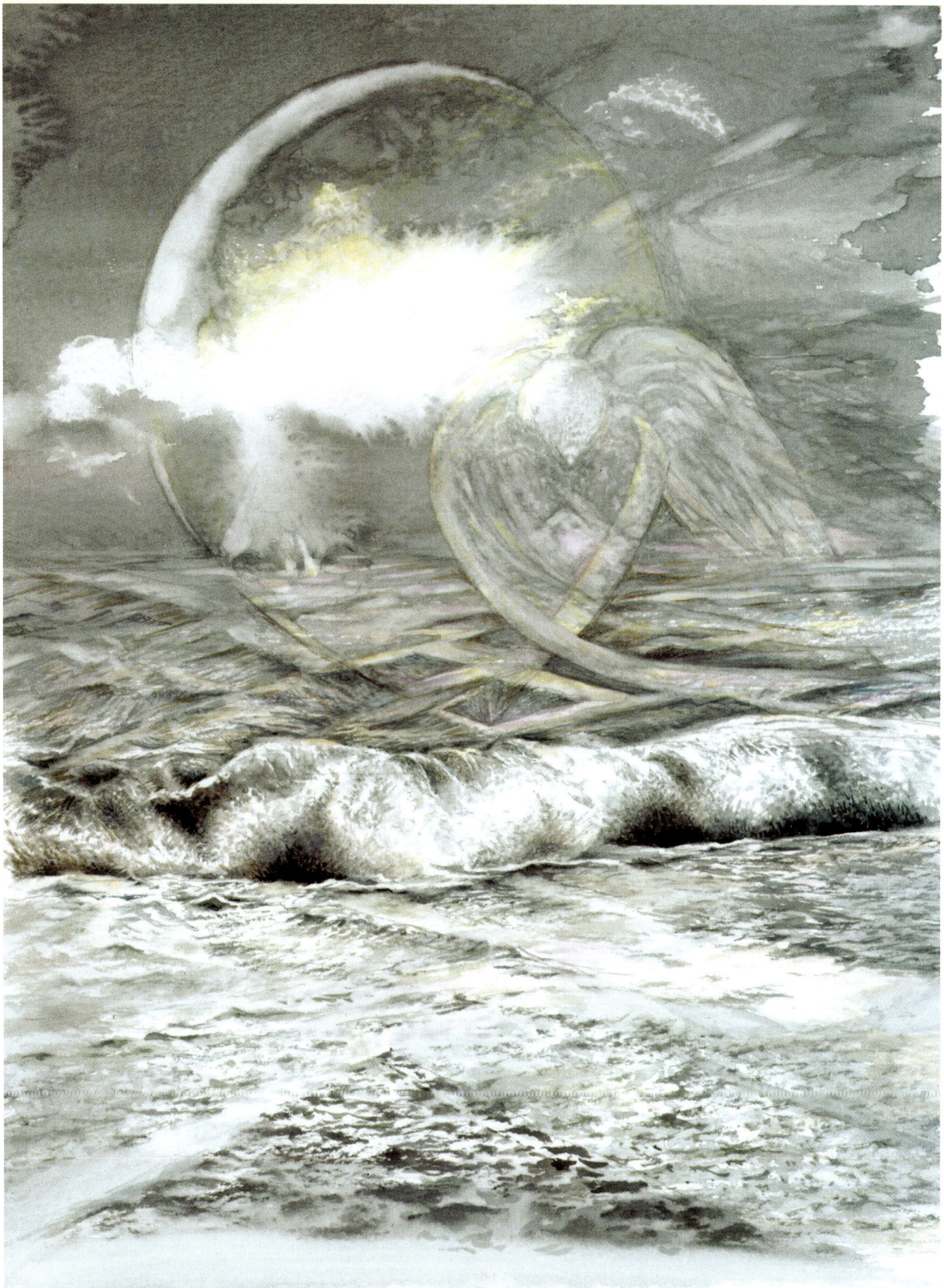

THE CROSS OF DECISION.

Standing in the Transept of Transition,
The Cross-Shaped Decision was before Me.
I felt the urge to walk straight on,
But beyond Its Waist, the Bridge narrowed
And vanished into Nothingness.

Confronted by the choice to Run Away,
Or stay in the strength of Stillness,
Mind and Spirit spiralled in Conflict.
Then in the Cross, a Presence emerged,
And took my Hands, saying
"Come, look not at the Problem with Logic
Rather seek in Symbols for Solution,
See in Shapes and Colours
What the Spirit Knows."
And as the Spirit spoke Its Truth,
These Images appeared.
In the Egg-Cupped grasp of my tight Hand
Was entombed a Soulless Circle of Gauze,
Flat and Still, Starched in a soundless Sea.
I shivered and tried to stir Its frozen Waves,
But they seemed suspended forever,
And I knew this was Not the place to Be.
But the Other Hand, that of Inspiration,
Reached into the depths of a rainbow River,
That flowed with the Force of rushing Colours
So strong, that I couldn't hold Its Power
As It raced through my fingers, and fell
As the light of exploding Stars.

And when my hands touched each other
In the black Hole, that cut into the Heart of Heaven,
They streamed through the haze of the Milky Way
Sparkling a Path of profound Certainty,
Back to their Birthing Place.

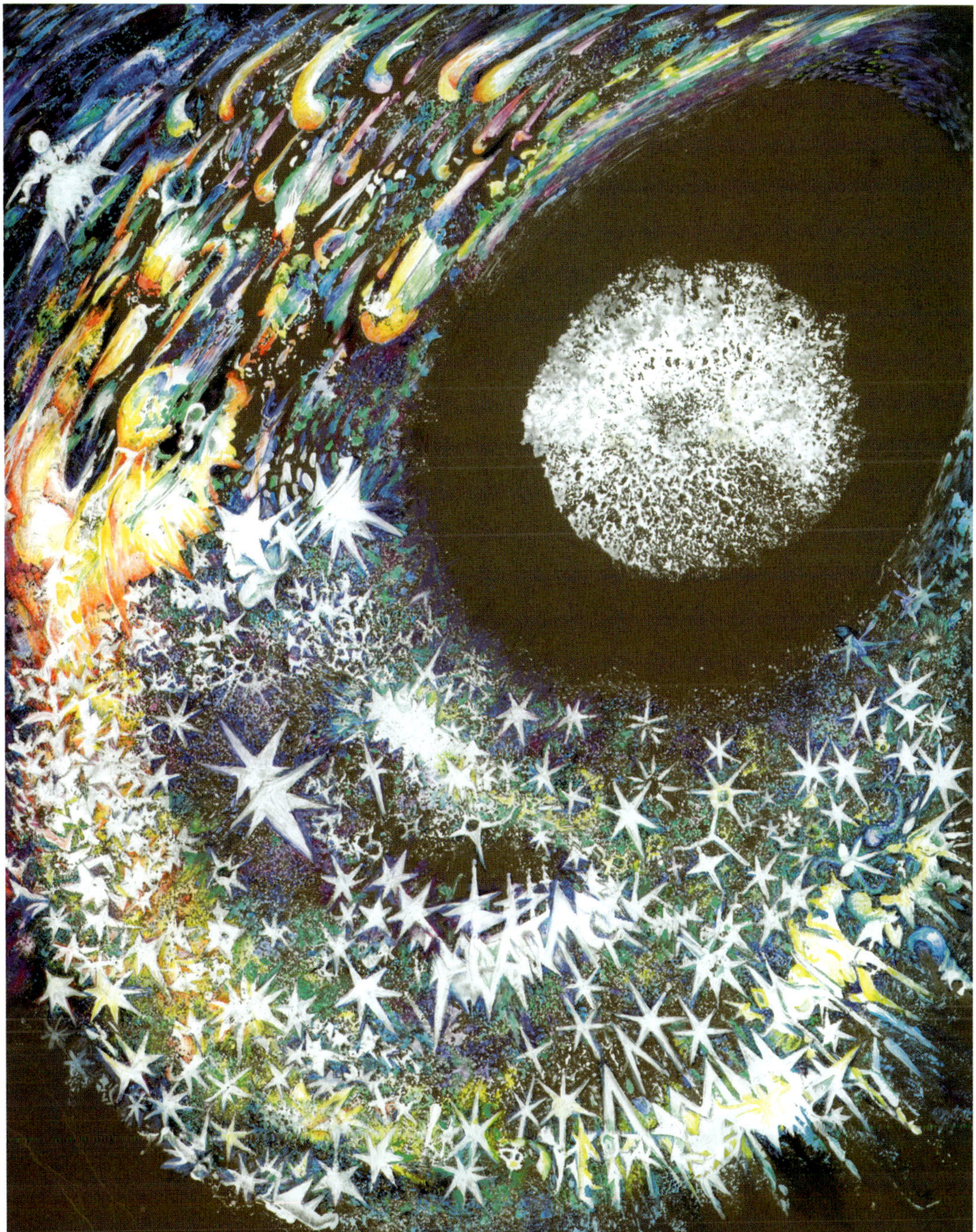

GREY AISLES.

TONIGHT,
It's like Crawling Through
The Roughness of Dry Grass.
Lost in Its Grey Aisles
I have no Direction,
But feel in Its Dryness
A Sound, a Movement .....
A Departing from Where I Am.
It seems like a Parting of our Ways,
And I stand in Emptiness
Hoping that the Movement will cease.
But even in the Silence I Create,
The Vibrations Know No End.
But Despite my Effort to be Still,
Their Energy Resonates forever,
There is such a Life Force Below,
Thrusting Up for lightness
Through the Depression of my Feet,
That I 'm Lifted to a Weightless State,
Where having No Substance
There is No Suppression of my Soul.
And I Hover Now
Above an infinite Field
Of Flowing Light,
Emotionless, Timeless and Eternal
As I Fall gently back
Into Its Ceaseless Rhythm.

What is Prayer
But a Sigh of Trust
Declaring in the Night
A need to take Thought
As to Who we Are
In this constant Hymn, that Sings
In the Vastness of the Universe.
What Is this Sound
That Vibrates in the Soul
To give Chorus to the Whole?
Why this Urge to "Come Together"?

POUNDED PEBBLE.

Torn away from a Distant Land
By the cruel Cull of Unseen Hands
I was carried Ashore by the weeping Waves;
A pounded Pebble, flattened to a shape
That I did not recognise, as Me.
There I was laid to Rest on a Granite Rock
Whose Time Worn Face, mocked the wooing Waters
Rejecting their bold Advances with Contempt
As they threw themselves in Temper at Its Feet.
And as they withdrew for their next Attack,
I clung Into Its immutable shape,
For it Seemed a secure Retreat,
A safe place to Contemplate
The perils of my journey back
Across the unmapped Space between Shore and Sky
Where Contours were changing constantly.
I gazed in terror at those tumbling Tunnels
Whose crumbled Trenches threatened to engulf Me.
And drenched in a Deluge of Doubts
I spoke into the Crevices of my Fear,
And the Rock held me close,
And sighed through wetted Lips,
"Much as I delight in your company,
The Tides will come and take you from me,
But be assured that I will Be with You,
For though we are of different Forms,
We come from the Same Source."
And in the Certainty of those Words
I surrendered in serenity
And slid back into the Sea,
Knowing that in The Taking,
Would Be my Transformation.

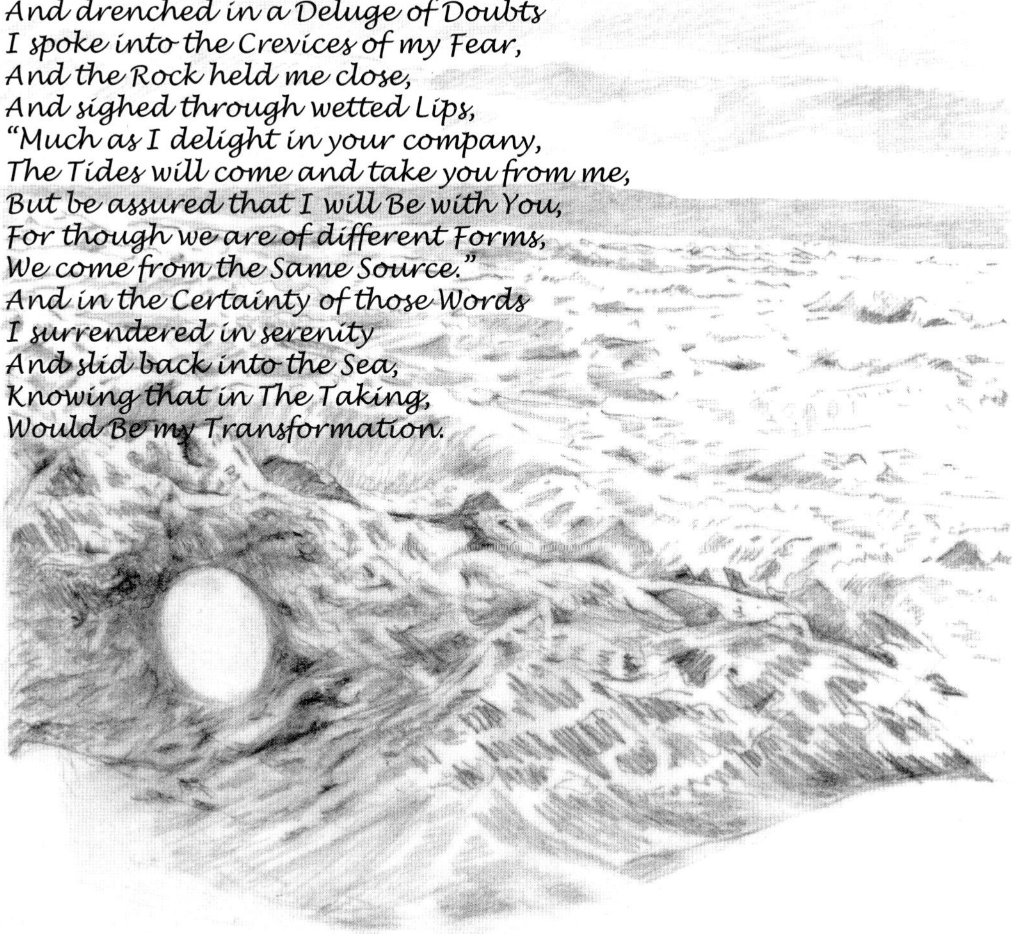

THE FABRIC OF BEING.

And I said to God,
Please Soften the Light,
Its too Bright,
I'm Blinded by Its Strength."
And without my Seeing
He Spread the Light so Far
Revealing Crevices in his Universe
That I had never been given Sight of Before.
And I said to God,
"Thankyou for Diffusing the Intensity,
For now I can look in Wonder
At the Hugeness of your Canvas
And not see just "The Bit that's Me."
Now I rest in Its Centre,
Rejoicing in Its Depths
As I see Its Wholeness.
So, Thankyou God,
For Softening the Light!

THE SLIPPER OF THE UNIVERSE.

And God Held Out his Hand,
And said, "Come,
And Walk With Me in Comfort."
And God showed to Me
His Slipper of the Universe,
And said, "When you chose
To Step Into Its Hugeness,
Then You will Know
The Depths of Your Soul,
And no longer need to Feel
The Hardness of the Earth
Beneath your Feet."
And I said to God,
"How do I Know that I will Fit In!"
And God Held my Feet
In the warmth of his Hands,
And Stretched his Universe
To say, "Come, walk With Me,
That I may enfold you
In my Wholeness."

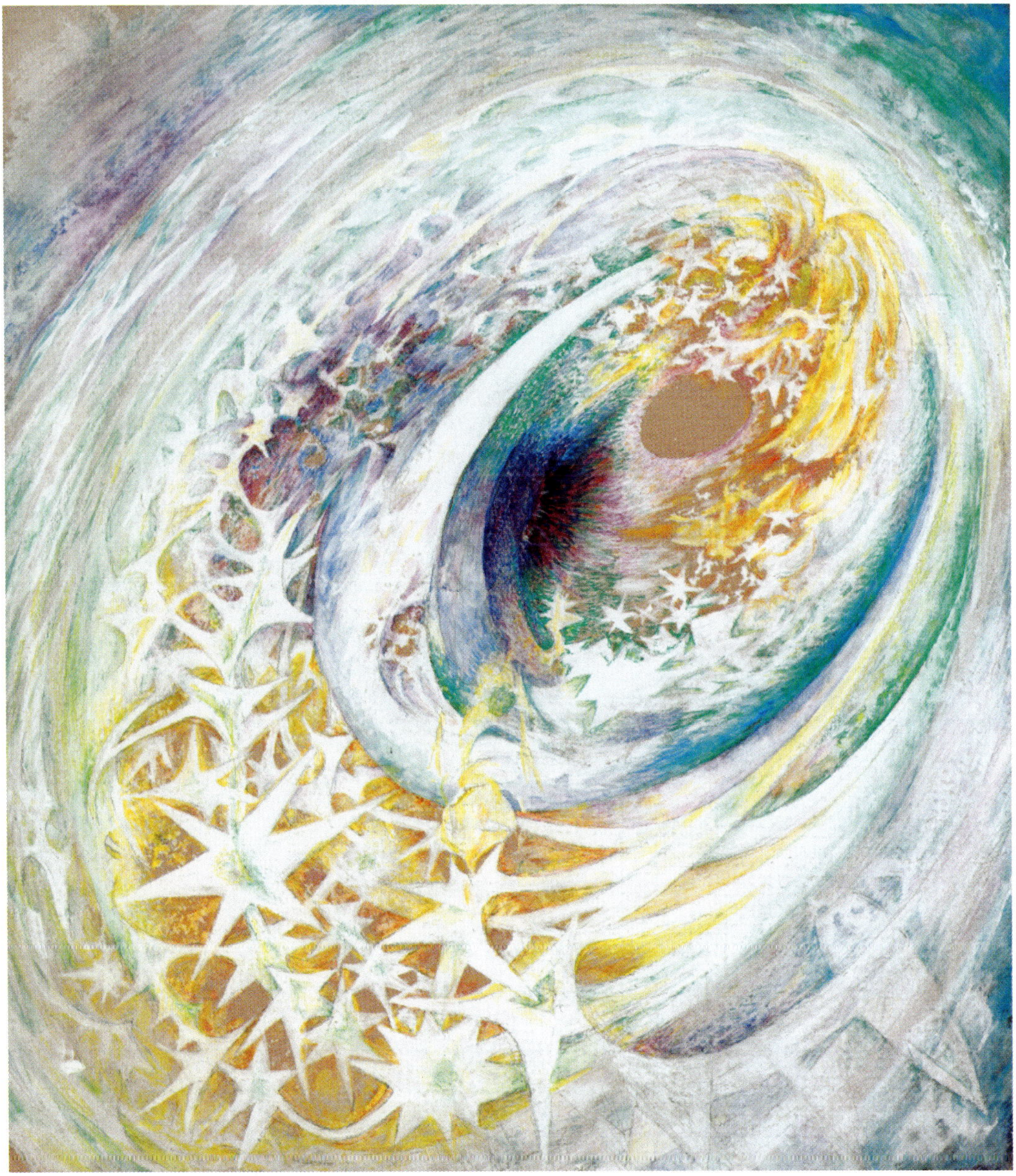

THE STAR OF THE UNIVERSE.

You are Not the Scattering Star,
Stranded in an empty Space
Of Your Own Making.
You Are the Centre
Of the Flowering Universe,
Your Feet Dance
In the Light of Ascent,
And the Dark of Descent,
For You Breath Out
And Back into the Centre.
In that perpetual Rhythm
There can be no End
To where you can Reach.

Beyond the Sky
There is an Outer Unknown,
Where we all Shine as Stars.
Beneath the Sky,
There is the Inner Unknown.
And There, we are Our Own Star
Shining Inside Out
As Universal Light.
Light is the Manifestation
Of our Awakening In Ourselves
To give that Light to Others.
Love is the Manifestation
Of our Forgiveness of Ourselves
To give Forgiveness to Others.
Laughter is the Manifestation
Of Rejoicing in Ourselves,
To give that Joy to Others.

THE FABRIC OF THE UNIVERSE.

And God said,
"I Spread Before You
The Fabric of My Universe.
And through the canopy of its Archways
I have Created Clusters of Stars
To Guide you on Your Way.
I have Formed the Earth along its Hem,
That in the Fullness of its Pockets
You may Feel My Presence
In All that Touches and Speaks
Through Your Senses.
And through the Open Spaces of the Heavens,
I draw Together All the Threads
That cloak my Mystery
But Know that Each Thread
Connects You To My Centre,
As I Draw You Back
Into the Depths of my Labyrinth
Through those Pitted Black Holes
That Are There to Refine Your Being
Into Purest Essence
And Though the Journey
May Seem without End, Know Always
That I Have marked a Pathway for You
In Beams of Glorious Light!"

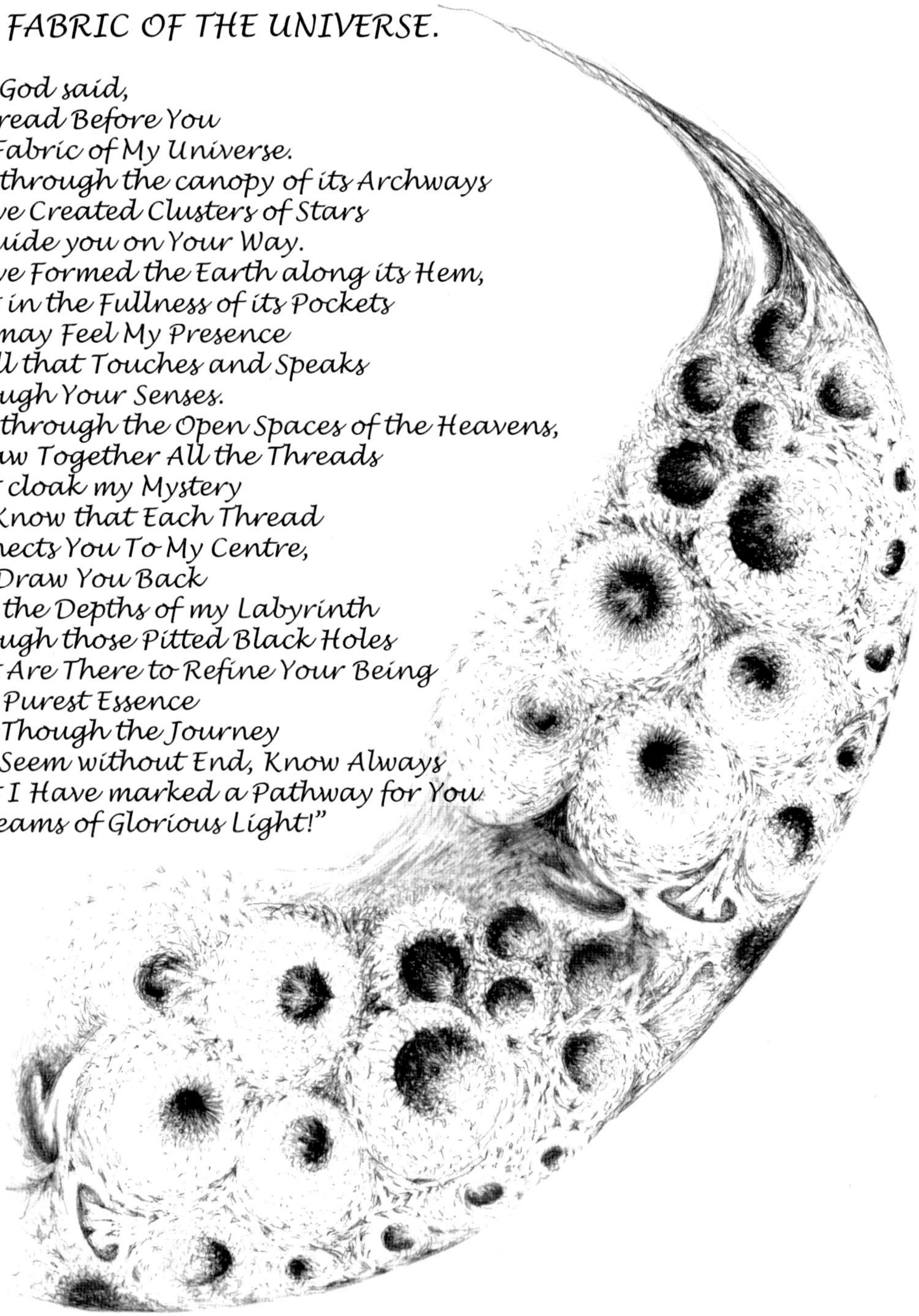

HIDDEN IN THE HELIX.

A Trusting Hand was laid in Mine,
And sandwiched in Its safety
I was asked, "Where are you Now,
For you have been so long away."
    And I replied, "I have travelled far
    Along my Shape, and return to give thanks
    For the Healing so softly held
    In the intertwined Helix, as It Unites,
    And departs again on Its repeating journey.
For there is no straight Pathway,
Rather a curved Outline of Its Form,
Before It returns to touch the Truth of Its Centre.
    And from Its given Strength,
    To flow upwards on Its Spiral,
    Knowing that in each Ascent
    It draws ever closer, until The Seed,
    Conceived in the intensity of Its Womb
    Opens, to reveal the beauty of Its Creation."

So even as Today was given
As an embrace at Our Centre
We know that as we depart on the Helix Path,
We will always be looking To Each Other.
    For as we reach Our Extremities,
    We will turn, and move Inwards
    To greet again In Our Centre.
For Love Is the Thread that holds the Helix
And draws us back Together,
And so it will ever Be.

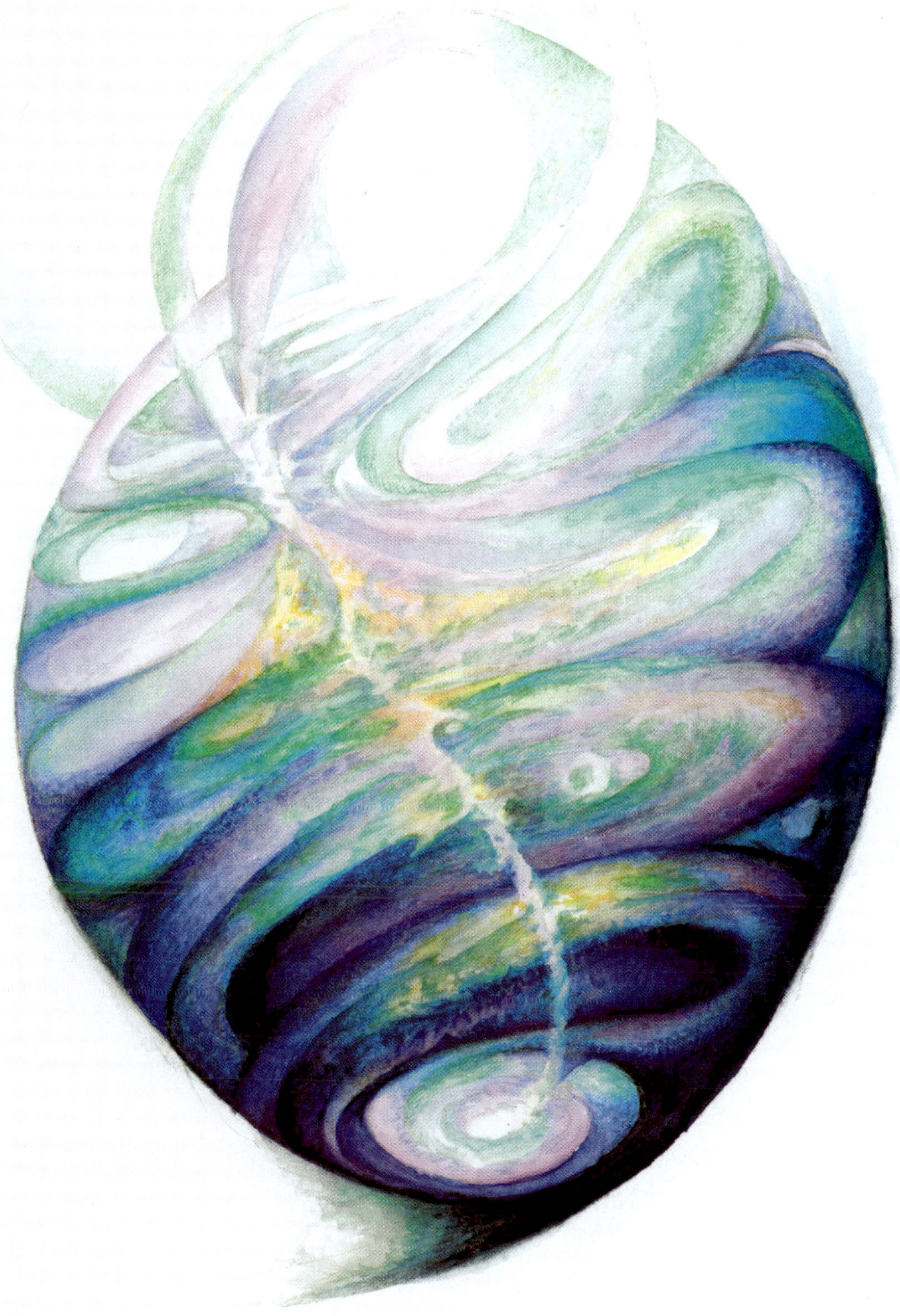

PLAYTIME.

As we run laughing into Playtime,
God enters the Classroom,
And writes on the White Board
With a Pen of White Light,
That makes his Message Invisible.
It's only when He calls us back in,
And closes the Door to Outside
And asks us to sit in the Darkness
With our Soul, that Then
His message is Revealed.
It is the Word, "LOVE",
That spirals out into the light,
And encircles us in Itself.

PARTY TIME.

As I asked in the Night,
I was invited to the Party
And saw the other Children
Receiving their Gifts of Empty Boxes
So beautifully wrapped in gaudy Paper.
    And I stood in the Corner watching
    As they processed by, and disappeared
    Into what they had received.
And the Giver walked towards Me, and said,
"Why did You not step forward
To Receive the Gift I have for You?"
    And I replied, "The Mountain of Gifts you Offered
    Seemed overwhelming, for all I wanted
    Was that small plain Package inscribed, Love,
    That lay Hidden under this Display."
And the Giver gazed at Me, and said,
"How glad I am in what you have chosen
For this Is my Real Gift to You, Open It
And find delight in Its simplicity."
    And as He departed in steps of Light,
    I knew what Joy would be mine
    In sharing each layer of Its unfolding.

BATH TIME.

Whatever Image of Love you give to Me,
Has the wonderful Indefinity
Of a Water Colour, Painted by the Soul.
For knowing that Water in Its Fluidity,
Is a Catalyst of Release,
You drew with Love from Its free flow
And stroking the tight stretched Paper's Face,
Brushed It gently to soothe Its tautness
With swathing washes of healing Hues.
    And in the running rays of Light Colours grew,
    Showering the Watery Field
    To reveal a Spectrum of bursting Flowers,
    That spreading into each other's shapes,
    Reformed as prisms of star tipped Spears
    To penetrate those tensioned Fibre Bars
    That guard the Gate to other Dimensions.
But the Stars faded, as in my need to find you
I dived through those revealing layers,
Not staying to absorb Into myself
The Images that they held.
So I arrive Breathless,
Compressed within those gloomy Depths,
Where sound and movement cease to Be.
    And resting in this timeless Tomb,
    I transmute into All those infinite Hues,
    As their Purity washed clean in the Waters,
    Become Again, as One.

BED TIME.

When the Time comes to Fullfilment,
The Heart can Break in Love,
And All Its facets,
Find a Resting Place
Within the Darkness of Others.
Love can never be Destroyed
If It Is A Truth
That needs to Spread Afar,
For Its Core is Always There,
Caring for Its many Shoots,
That Grow and Glow, to Lighten
The Dull World of Others.

THE ROSE TREE.

Love is not about Sentimentality,
But about a deep Need to Reveal
The Nature of God
Within Ourselves.
So You Are In My Being,
Not as a Thorn,
But as The Essence
Of the Rose Tree.
For Pain And Pleasure
ARE the Duality of Love.

So, The Depth and the Height
Of my Love For You
Goes Beyond this Dimension,
Out of Self, and Into Being.
There are no Barriers
Between Roles,
In Accepting, and being Accepted,
Loving, and being Loved,
For we Transform constantly
In those Different Aspects
Of Our Being.
We Are constant Companions,
As the Sun is to the Moon.
To Be Light in the Dark,
And Dark in the Light,
And so we will continue to Evolve,
Until we resolve the Uniting
Of both those Aspects,
Into One.

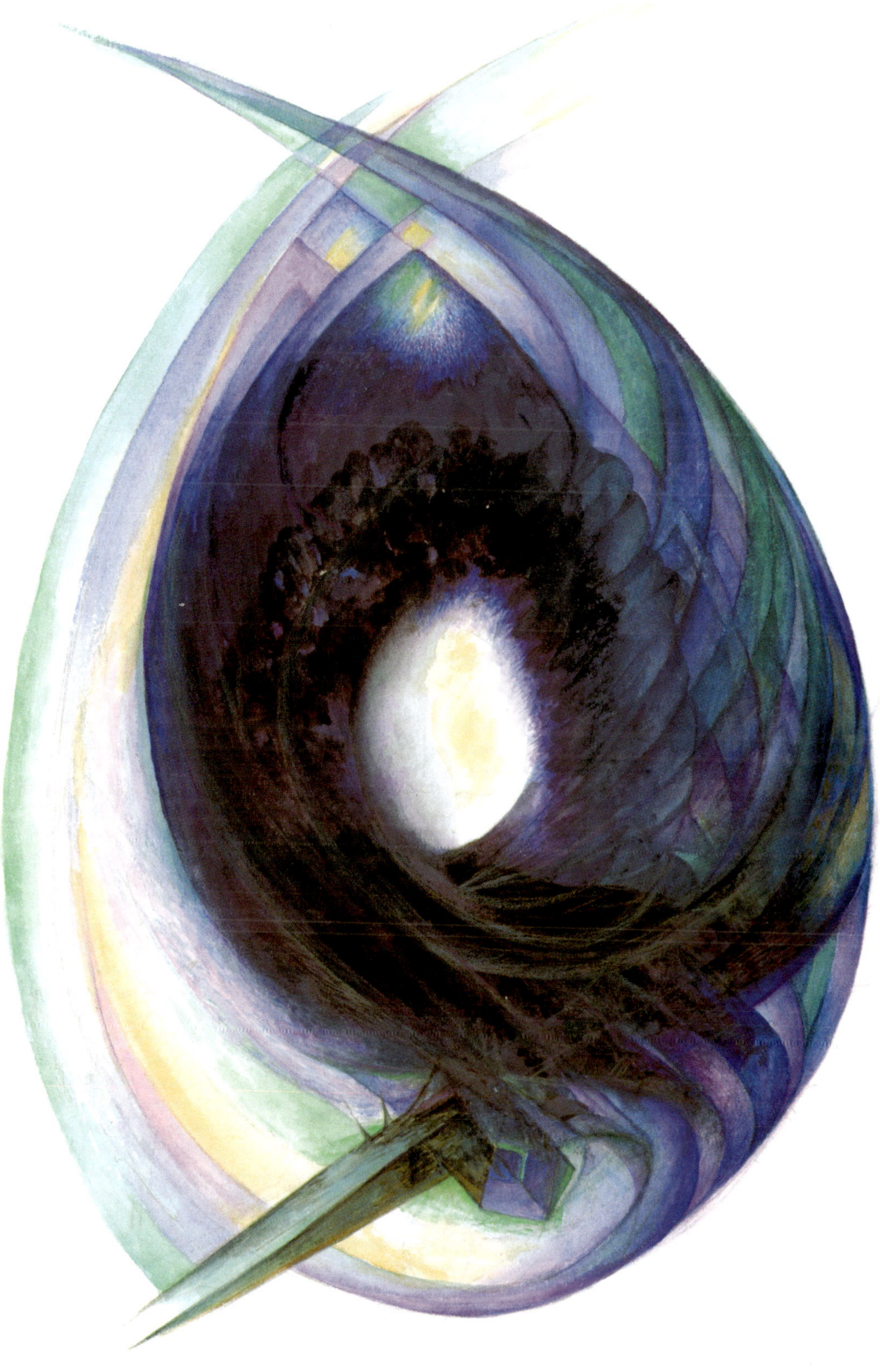

ME, AND MY SHADOW.

Anchored by our Shadows,
How precious are those moments,
When Talking in the Wind,
And Speaking with the Sea,
We share those words spoken in Silence.
Even as your Breath Departs,
Hear my Breath come Into You..
And even as you breath In again,
Hear my breath passing through You
To enter the Centre of Love.
And Know,
That in that constant Interchange,
Is the Essence of Being.

But Know too,
That though our Souls Touch
In the Shadows that they Cast,
Our Lightness
Is forever Our Own,
Of the same Essence,
But unique in Its Own Shape.
Though our Souls Touch
In the Shape that they Are,
Our Shape
Is forever Our Own,
Of the same Essence,
But unique in Its Own Shape.

And if that Shape is Violated
Bt the Penetration of Another,
Then its Own Shape Disintegrates
Into that Ocean of Infinite Essence
Where Transformed, It flows
Into the Kaleidoscope of Shapes
That move within the Structure
Of God's Re-Formation,
And so It will Ever Be.

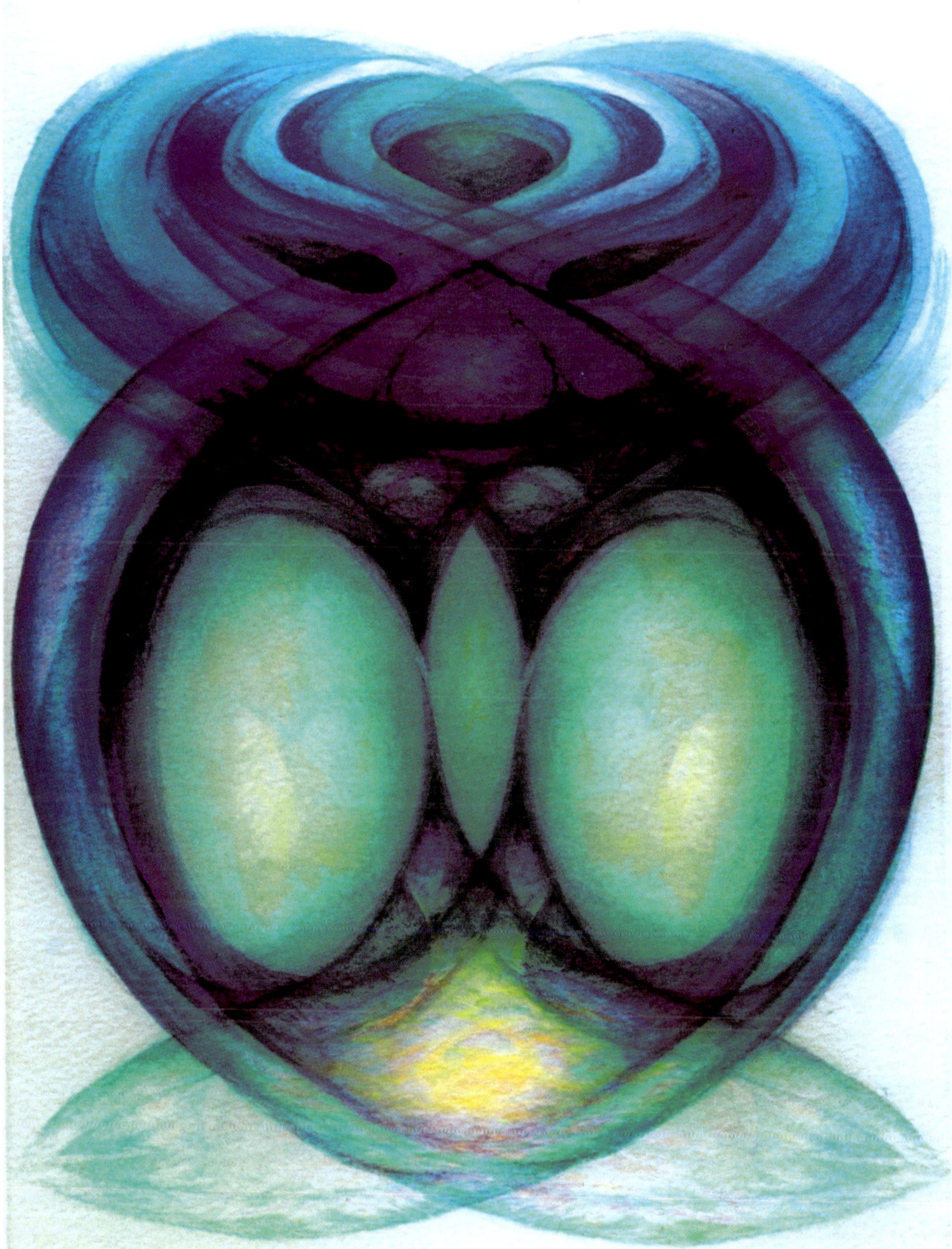

THE TAIL END OF TODAY.

At the Tail End of Today, Tomorrow peers
And Disappears Into Itself.
In Today, I have come this solitary way
Through a Labyrinth of tightening Circles,
And when I arrived in Its Centre
I asked, "Where do I Go Now?"
Outside the Universe stayed silent,
And held Its Breath that the Inner Breath
Could speak in the deep Centre of Being.
"Listen Only to what I say,
For then you will Know where you Are,
And in that fleeting Glimpse of Truth,
You will BE Where you Are.
For you Are in constant Transition
And can Only BE in the Now.
So waste not your Vitality
In Projecting Forward,
For you can only Anticipate,
Not BE in the Future.
Turn Into the Shadows of Yesterday,
For they have Clouded your Being.
NOW is The Time to turn round
And Face those Granite Rocks
That Block the Entrance to your Past,
And Direct your Energies
Into Lightening those dark Recesses
Where Fear has Hoarded Itself.
Expel It, Dispel It, Bid It Farewell
And BE in the Duality of the Present,
Where Past and Future Unite
At the Point of NOW!"

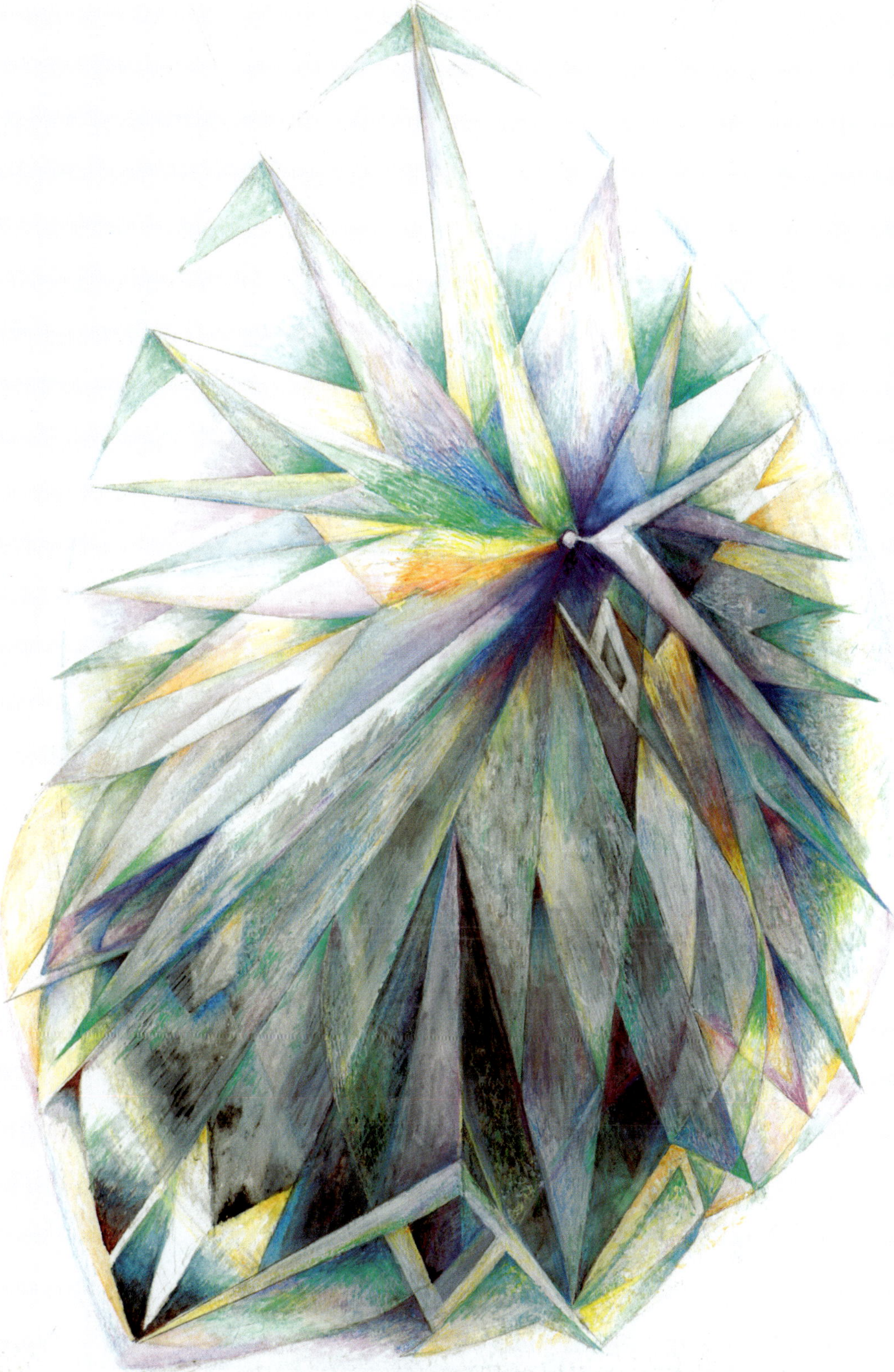

THE TIMELESS JOURNEY.

In the Mirrored Reflection
Of the Infinite Image,
We are forever Rebirthed ,
As mighty Waves of Light
Emerging from the Chaos of Creation
To surge across the Rainbow Bridge
That communes between Heaven and Earth.
The Wave I Be, as "Me",
Is in The Second, NOW.
Knowing that in the Vitality
Of Its flowering Strength,
It holds the Agony and the Ecstasy
Of being denied the Power
To sustain Its Substance.
And as Its swelling Shape Breaks,
Disintegrates, and Dies, It is taken
By the Tribulations of the Tide; to turn,
Transformed ,on Its return to the Horizon
From whence It came.
This is a place of Mystery,
The Resonance of Eternal Tunes,
The dark Womb of Infinity;
Where in the Breath of Shadowed Presence
The Creator awaits Our Coming,
That in the Agony and Ecstasy of Love,
We are Re-Formed, and Born again,
In a different Shape and Size,
But Forever, of the Same Essence.

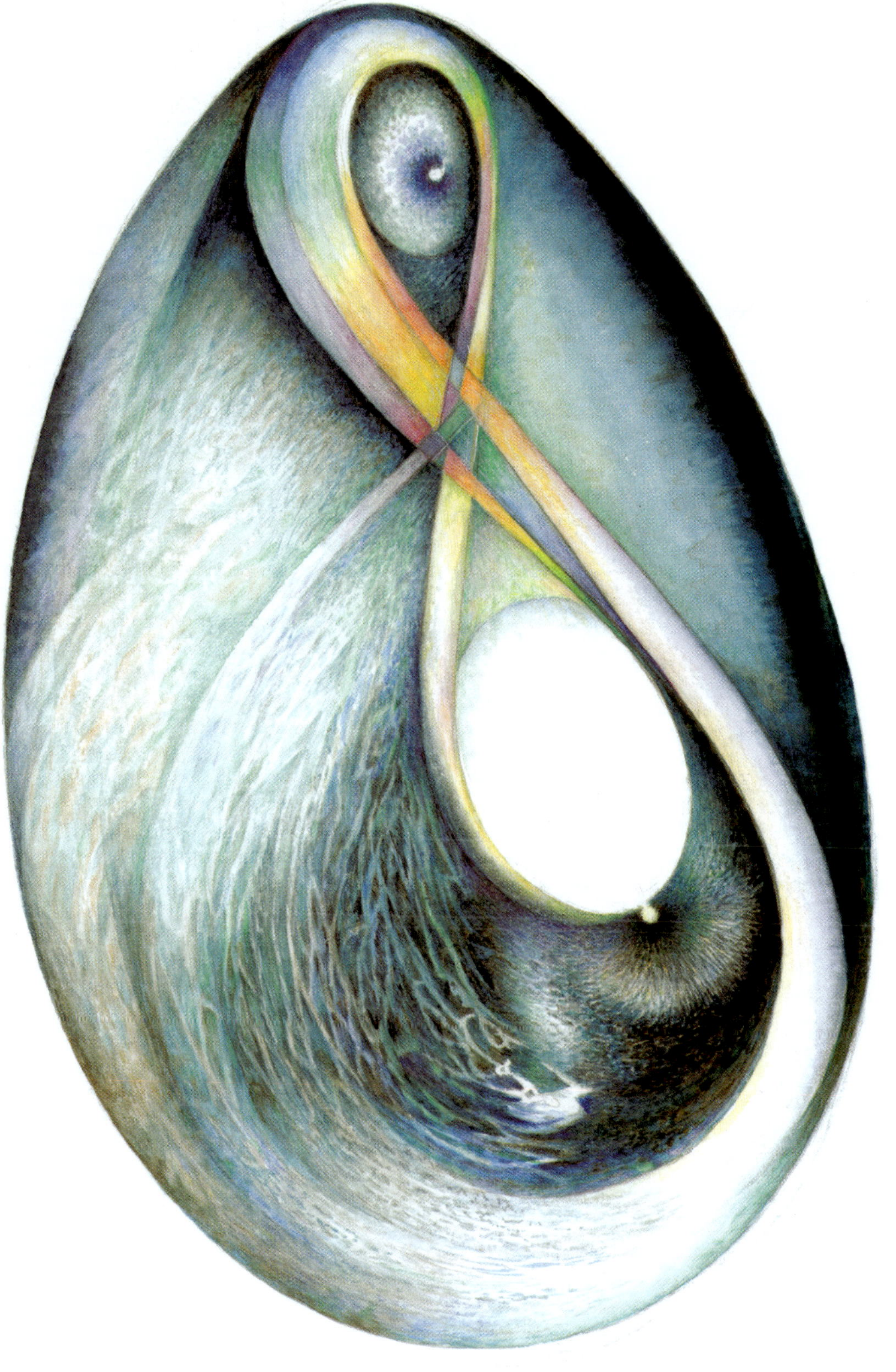

AT THE END OF THE DAY!

When a Million "BITS OF FUN,"
And a Million "BITES OF HURT,"
Are Glued Together
To Make a Picture of The Day,
Then all we can do is Laugh!
        But the odd Bit, or Bite
        That won't Stick
        Makes such a Difference
        To the Uniting
        Of Joy and Despair
        Into a Complete Image.
At the End of the Day, how I Wish
That I could Glue Together
The "Right" Number of "Bits and Bites",
For then I could Laugh in Delight,
And Sleep at Peace with Myself!
                For we give to others
                That which we need to Receive
                For Our Self.
                Too Often, we Expect too Much
                Of those not yet ready to Share,
                But that should Never allow us,
                In Our Own Hurt, to say to Self,
"I won't Give" for then the Soul Rebukes Us.
                Reminding us that what we Hold,
Is Not Ours to Give,
                Only to Pass On!
At the End of the Day
We needs Turn Round,
And read the Lesson that It Gave.
        To Cry in Delight at the Beauty
        Of Special Moments.
        To Laugh in Forgiveness at the Pain
        Of Unfeeling Hurt.
To Speak in Understanding,
As a companion to the contented Soul.
To Sing in Happiness with an Unheard Chorus,
That Proclaims,
That what we Learn in Each day
Is a Preparation for Our Last Day.
        So Smile as You Read the Words,
        And Turn then, to Rest in Comfort
        With what This Day Provided!

WHAT'S THE PURPOSE?

I have been asked
To stay in the Quietness of God's Purpose,
But Do find the Silence so hard to bear,
When All I hear is my Soul
Crying out for a Companion,
To share the Gifts God gave Me.
In this Stillness, where Nothing Moves
Please give Me the Strength
To Hold my Back Always Straight.
Please give Me the Understanding
To Bow my Head, when Pressured
By the Energies from Without and Within.
Please give Me the Trust
That they will find Balance with each other.
And Please, give Me the Wisdom
In this Empty place to Know My Purpose.

AND GOD REPLIED.

In "NOW" You can never Grow Old,
For you Are in Infinity
Where there is no Concept of Time or Space
To Confine you Immortal Soul.
It Is a place of Clarity
In the Shadow of Mystery
Where I Gave You Life.
And with that Life, I gave My Love,
And gave You too
Free Choice of Its Expression.
In "NOW", You begin to Perceive
How You Starved Its Growth
By holding It tight into your Self.
In "NOW," You know Its need to be Free
From the deep Wound of your suffering,
That it may Open Out for All to See.
I Created You for That Purpose!
And "NOW," I beseech
That in That Understanding,
You give Me your Companionship,
For I can only BE-Come,
If you let Me Come
Into the Life I gave You."

11.11.03.

Marion,
with love
& light,
As ever
Yvonne.